Poland

Front cover: Gdańsk harbour
Right: Horse-drawn carriage in
Kraków

TOP 10 ATTRACTIONS

Kraków The former capital of Poland is still the country's artistic and cultural centre and its most popular tourist destination (page 34)

Wieliczka Salt Mines With its extraordinary, ornately carved chambers, this Unesco World Heritage Site is a must-see (page 57)

Tatra Mountains With spectacular peaks they a hiker's paradise (page 6

Warsaw A truly capital where history and cultu come alive (page 71)

Zamość Modelled on Italian trading cities, the Old Town is a 16th-century Renaissance jewel (page 68)

Gdańsk The birthplace of the Solidarity Movement (page 92)

Sopot Poland's lively summer capital (page 102)

Malbork Castle Built by the Teutonic Knights and one of Europe's biggest strongholds (page 104)

Kazimierz Dolny A confection of Renaissance and Mannerist houses (page 70)

Kazimierz Kraków's former Jewish quarter is re-inventing itself while not forgetting its past (page 150)

A PERFECT TOUR

Day 1 Wawel hill

Discover some of Poland's greatest treasures on Kraków's Wawel hill. Tour the Royal Castle first, have lunch in Kawiarnia Pod Baszta in the visitor centre, then see the cathedral where Poland's kings were crowned. Catch a short classical concert in one of the Old Town churches before dinner at Kraków's oldest restaurant, Wierzynek (see page 149).

Day 2 Students and synagogues

Soak up the atmosphere of this ancient university city at Café Camelot (see page 147) on Rynek Główny. Then head to Kazimierz, once the Jewish quarter, where ancient synagogues now sit side by side with edgy cafés and clubs.

Day 3 Medieval mall

Spend the morning souvenir-searching in the Sukiennice, Kraków's medieval market building, before heading to Warsaw by internal flight or train.

Day 4 Warsaw rebuilt

From the top of the Soviet Palace of Culture you get an excellent view of Warsaw's modern skyscrapers and rebuilt Old Town. Take a tram to the Warsaw Rising Museum and then walk east through former ghetto streets, for a more light-hearted afternoon in the Old Town, taking lunch in the Rynek Starego Miasta, and visiting the Historical Museum of Warsaw.

Day 5 Royal route

See more of old Warsaw today by visiting the Royal Castle in the morning then taking a slow stroll down from Plac Zamkowy, passing Warsaw University, and stopping for a visit to the National Museum or the Chopin Museum and taking a break for a coffee or a bite to eat on elegant Nowy Świat.

OF POLAND

Day 7   Historic Toruń

Walk around the medieval city walls to see Toruń's leaning tower, then visit the museum where its most famous son, Copernicus, was born, and marvel at the stars in its Planetarium. In the evening hear live folk music as you eat at Karczma Spichrz (see page 153).

Day 6   Scenic palace

Take a trip to downtown Warsaw to admire the beautiful Łazienki Palace and enjoy an afternoon strolling in the peaceful gardens, where locals come to relax. Later, take the train to Toruń.

Day 8   Malbork Castle

An early train from Toruń Główny will get you to Malbork in less than three hours. Spend the day exploring the castle, the massive brick stronghold of the Teutonic Knights, before taking an early evening train to Gdańsk. Dine at the riverside Restauracja Baryłka (see page 152).

Day 9   On the waterfront

Get the Hanseatic flavour of the Main Town by following the Royal Route from Upland Gate to Golden Gate, before plunging into more recent history at the Solidarity Museum, near the famous shipyards. Dine back in old Gdańsk at Restauracja Targ Rybny (see page 153) in the fishmarket.

Day 10   Beach life

Frequent trains from Gdańsk will take you to lovely seaside resort of Sopot. Here you can relax on the beach, take a walk along its pier or explore the many nature trails in the area by bike or on foot. Eat at Bulaj (see page 153) on the beach and enjoy the laidback atmosphere.

CONTENTS

48

64

86

88

76

142

INTRODUCTION

Even though the country is more than 1,000 years old, Poland's survival is something of a miracle. Its boundaries were continually redrawn over the course of eight centuries. Then suddenly the nation disappeared from the map. Between 1795 and 1918, Poland, wedged in the middle of Europe, ceased to exist for the world's cartographers. Partitioned for a third time at the end of the 18th century by Prussia, Austria and Russia, Poland was reduced to a promise and a prayer for Poles, and the object of tug-of-war for more powerful states.

But that was only one aspect of Poland's troubles; then the real tragedy occurred. Hitler and the Nazis invaded Poland, launching World War II, then extinguished many of its cities and eradicated 20 percent of its people, including nearly its entire Jewish population of three-and-a-half million – until then the largest Jewish community in Europe. Wars have befallen many countries in modern times, but few have been as thoroughly ravaged as Poland.

Yet Poland rebuilt itself from the rubble of war. From photographs, paintings, architectural drawings and the memories of its grief-stricken survivors, Poles reconstructed the Old Towns of Warsaw and Gdańsk brick by brick, only to suffer four decades of Soviet-imposed Communist rule and grudging submission behind the Iron Curtain. Yet Poland asserted itself once more.

In the 1980s, the trade union movement Solidarity (Solidarność) helped to trigger the demise of Communism in Poland and throughout the Soviet bloc. Poland has survived with its culture, language, spirit and most of its territory intact, and in 2004 it joined the European Union, as a modern, independent nation.

The Podhale region and the Tatra mountains

Historic Cities

Largely rural, Poland has great tracts of wilderness and primeval forest in its 22 national parks. However, the country is perhaps best known for ancient towns rich in history and architecture. Kraków, which survived unscathed from the war, is a splendid medieval city (it was the royal capital for 500 years), with a magnificent market square, castle complex on a hill, and one of Europe's oldest, most prestigious universities.

Warsaw, Poland's largest city by far and its commercial and political capital, is not the bleak grey morass of Communist days. It may still be a little harsh on the eyes in places, but it is undeniably beautiful in others, and perhaps best expresses Poland's current crossroads. A 20-minute walk can take you from the Royal Castle to a monolith of Stalinist architecture to the gleaming headquarters of international companies banking on Poland's emergence as a major European player.

While Warsaw's Old Town is an astonishing phoenix-like fable of reconstruction, Gdańsk's historic centre is even more alluring, its Royal Way a loving restoration that defies the imagination. No matter how many times you stroll through the medieval layouts of these cities over cobblestoned streets, gazing at stunning examples of Gothic, Renaissance and Baroque architecture created, incredibly, as late as 1953, you cannot help but be amazed. The buildings look genuinely old; it is as though the indefatigable Polish people willed their authenticity.

Smaller towns can be just as impressive. Zamość is a perfect Renaissance town with one of the most photogenic main squares in the country. Zakopane is an Alpine-style town carved out of wood at the foot of the High Tatras, the highest peaks of the Carpathian Mountains, within easy range of great hiking and skiing. Toruń, the home of the great astronomer Nicolaus Copernicus, is a feast of red-brick Gothic architecture, while Poznań, a determined trade centre, combines commerce with authenticity in its extraordinary Old Market Square.

Population and Religion

Poland is a nation of a little under 39 million, the size of Spain. Its people are fervently Catholic – over 80 percent call themselves practising Catholics – and more conservative than many of their Western European neighbours. Throughout most of its history, Poland was an intensely cosmopolitan place, with Germans, Jews, Lithuanians, Belarusians, Armenians and others living within its borders. During the Second Republic (1919–39), only two-thirds of its people were ethnic Poles. It has also traditionally been a land of religious tolerance. When medieval Europe was rocked by religious wars, Poland was a safe haven for Jewish, Protestant and Orthodox refugees – making the intolerance later inflicted by Germany on Polish territory all the more terrible.

Today, Poland is unusually homogenous in terms of ethnicity: some 98 percent of the people are Poles. The Jewish population

More than 80 percent of Poles are practising Catholics

was reduced to 250,000 after World War II, and today there are only a few thousand Jews living in Poland. The largest minority groups are Lithuanians, Ukrainians and Belarusians.

Literacy rates are high, at a shade under 100 percent. Poles are well-educated, and young people in the larger cities speak English (much more so than German or Russian) with the same fluency and enthusiasm of those a couple of border lines west. They're up-to-date on fashions, trends and music; they have mobile phones glued to their ears and e-mail accounts they tap into daily at internet cafés across the country.

Rural Poland

Of course, the vast Polish countryside is a very different story. Here you'll still see a stubbornly traditional way of life that seems years, if not decades, slower than city life. Roads seldom bothered by cars are lined with wooden shrines, erected by

Exploring the squares of Warsaw

people intent on manifesting their devotion. Even if you're not planning on travelling through the countryside, you can get a good taste of rural life by visiting a skansen, or

Green Poland

Almost one third of Poland is covered by forest, mostly pine, spruce and mixed deciduous and coniferous trees.

outdoor ethnographic museum, which makes the ways of Polish country life accessible by relocating historic houses and farm buildings from small villages to open-air exhibitions.

A Blend of East and West

Poland's history as a territory coveted by great powers all around it ensured that the north–south divisions often seen elsewhere are, here, primarily east–west divisions. The west is more Germanic, organised, pragmatic and industrious, while the East has a reputation of being more Russian – which means, in short, relaxed, cultural and introspective. Poznań, for example, halfway between Berlin and Warsaw, revels in its business skills and organisational attitude. Kraków, the ancient capital much closer to Ukraine than Germany, is just as proud of its free-flowing cultural prowess and its status as a place where art and education override business (except, of course, for the business of tourism).

There has always been a cultural struggle between East and West in Poland. The Poles are a Slavic people, like their Ukrainian and Russian neighbours to the east. Yet their historical and cultural connections to the West are formidable. The Catholic Poles first took their religious cues from the West in the 10th century, and cultural epochs basic to Western Europe – the Enlightenment and the Renaissance, for example – were just as much a part of Polish society. The shared identity, as well as the uneasy conflicts, between East and West, have defined this land in ways that go far beyond geography.

A Nation of Triumphs

Although Poland has suffered a chequered political past, it has been the source of glorious achievements in the arts and sciences. Poland claims such greats as the composer Frédéric Chopin, the novelist Joseph Conrad, Marie Curie (Nobel Prize winner in chemistry and physics) and the Nobel Prize winners in literature Henryk Sienkiewicz, Władysław Reymont, Wisława Szymborska and Czesław Miłosz. In 1932 the country was the first to crack Germany's Enigma code, a feat many believe to have shortened World War II by at least three years and to have prevented a nuclear holocaust in Europe.

Life Post-Communism

Though by most measures, Poland, along with Hungary and the former Czech Republic, has made incredible strides in the years since the break-up of Communist Europe in 1989, many of its citizens and international institutions feel that

Chopin

Frédéric Chopin (1810–49) was born in Żelazowa Wola, just outside Warsaw, to a French father and Polish mother. He spent his youth in the capital but also learned all the folk songs and dances of the surrounding villages, which he utilised in almost all his later works. He made his debut as a classical pianist when still a boy, playing in elegant salons. In the autumn of 1830, he left Warsaw, then a small, autonomous duchy (though ultimately under the control of the Russian Tsar) and when the Russians occupied the duchy the following year, Chopin settled in Paris. In 1836 he met the novelist George Sand, who looked after him during his years of ill health, and he travelled with her to Majorca. His health continued to deteriorate, however, so he returned to France. In 1847, George Sand left him. Lonely, ill and poor, he fled to London, where he gave his last public performance. Returning to Paris, he died of tuberculosis.

the transition to privatisation and democracy has not been as smooth or as rapid as might have been hoped. Immediately after gaining political and economic freedom in 1989, Poland found itself without state support, and production plummeted. While there was a huge spurt in growth and prosperity in the mid-1990s, unemployment has recently increased

The spa town of Jelenia Góra

dramatically. However, with Poland now a member of the European Union (EU), the gap between Western and Central Europe is at last closing.

Yet Poles remember the past and the often-fractured road that has brought them to this point. They are intensely proud that Copernicus, who 'stopped the sun and moved the Earth' and revolutionised the way we understand our universe, was a Pole. They revel in the fact that Poland signed the second-oldest Constitution delineating government powers, after the United States. Poles young and old live with the horrors of death-camp atrocities committed on their soil. They turned out in great adoring hordes for the late Pope John Paul II, known to them as Karol Wojtyła, former Archbishop of Kraków. And the Polish people recognise the role that a little-known shipyard electrician in Gdańsk by the name of Lech Wałęsa had, first as a leader of the Solidarity union and then as Poland's first elected president since 1922, in indelibly changing the events of the second half of the 20th century. Poland may only now be developing as a destination for many of the world's travellers, but it is certainly no stranger to the world stage.

A BRIEF HISTORY

Poland's war-torn, almost incomprehensibly fractured history plays out like an epic novel – occasionally triumphant, frequently sad and tragic. Over a millennium, Poland evolved from a huge, economically powerful kingdom to a partitioned nation that ceased to exist on world maps for over 120 years, and finally to a people and land at the centre of the 20th century's greatest wars and most horrific human tragedies. But Poland has survived, with its culture, language and most of its territory intact, and today Poles, who entered into the European Union (EU) in 2004 and NATO in 1999, are taking their place at the forefront of post-Communist Central Europe.

Foundations of the Polish State

The region that would become Poland, a great plain sandwiched between the Wisła (Vistula) and Odra (Oder) rivers, has been inhabited since the Stone Age by migratory tribal peoples – among them Celts, Balts, Huns, Slavs and Mongols. Tribal culture reigned, untouched by the more sophisticated civilisation of the Roman Empire. Slavic tribes arrived by the 8th century AD and put down roots; the Ślężanie, Mazowszanie, Pomorzanie and Wiślanie peoples inhabited much of the territory. The Polonian tribe, which settled the area that today is western Poland around Poznań, provided the foundations for the development of a Polish language and nation.

Prince Mieszko, leader of the Piast dynasty that ruled the Polonians, undertook the bold step of unifying the Polanie and neighbouring tribes. Mieszko adopted

What's in a name?

The Polanie tribe (the Polonians), who lived in the Warta valley not far from Poznań, may have been the people who gave Poland its name. Polanie means 'of the fields'.

Christianity – probably an astute political move to place the new state on equal footing with nearby Christian states with ties to Rome – and married a Czech princess, Dobrawa, in 965. His religious conversion won him the support of the papacy, and Mieszko effectively founded the Polish state the following year. By the end of the 10th century, he had united his tribal territory, Wielkopolska (Great Poland), with that of another tribe, Małopolska (Little Poland) – regional names that remain in use today. Silesia, settled by a different tribe, would eventually become the third component of the nascent Polish state.

Stained-glass window, Franciscan Church, Kraków

Mieszko's son Bolesław 'The Brave' was acknowledged by Otto III, the Holy Roman Emperor. Bolesław later repelled invasions from Otto's successor and then sought Poland's own expansion eastwards; he eventually annexed parts of present-day Ukraine. The Pope recognised Bolesław as the first king of Poland in 1025, elevating the country to full membership in a European community of Christian states.

In between several often short, troubled and feuding reigns, Kazimierz I 'the Restorer' put the country on a firm footing again and established his court in Kraków. Kraków grew in importance and became the country's capital, replacing Gniezno in 1038. Kraków was better positioned for trade and also less vulnerable to attacks from the Czechs and Germans. Helped by the arrival of immigrants from all over Europe, including thousands of Jews, Kraków became a prosperous and culturally enriched capital.

From the mid-13th century, Tartars invaded Poland on three occasions. Threatened by the Prussians, Duke Konrad of Mazovia invited in the Order of the Teutonic Knights to help defend against them. The Knights used their considerable military might to then assume control of the very territory they had helped defend, capturing Gdańsk, securing most of the Baltic region and cutting off the rest of Poland from access to the sea. The Tartars defeated the Poles at the Battle of Legnica in 1241 and destroyed most of Kraków, leaving only the castle and St Andrew's Church intact.

Kazimierz the Great and the Jagiellonians
The last king of the Piast dynasty, Kazimierz III, the Great, succeeded in reunifying Poland. His rule ushered in Poland's

The Teutonic Knights

The Teutonic Knights were a military order of German knights who served in the Holy Land. They played an important part in Polish history, originally acquiring their prosperity through gifts of land for their hospital work during the Crusades. They were also given land in northeast Poland in 1225 in return for assisting the Mazovian Duke Konrad to repel an invasion of pagan Prussians. After annexing this Prussian territory, they gradually extended their occupation, invading Polish towns such as Gdańsk in the early 14th century and slaughtering the inhabitants, until their incursions were finally repulsed by the joint Polish-Lithuanian Commonwealth, and the knights were defeated in 1410 at the Battle of Grunwald. Malbork Castle (see page 104), established as the headquarters of the Knights' grand master, was taken over by the Poles in 1457 and the grand master swore allegiance to the Polish king.

first golden age. Kazimierz built great castles and towns, codified laws, and created an entire administrative system of governance for the war-torn country. He rebuilt Kraków with magnificent architecture and established the country's first university there. Kazimierz, a pragmatist, did not try to wrest control of Silesia, in the hands of Bohemia, or the territory seized by the independent state of the Teutonic Knights. Instead, he consolidated the state by expanding eastwards and accepting minority populations, including persecuted Jews from across Europe, into the predominantly Catholic nation.

Malbork Castle

Kazimierz's death in 1370 left the crown to his nephew, Louis of Anjou, the King of Hungary. One of his daughters, Jadwiga, succeeded Louis in Poland, while the other assumed control of Hungary. Jadwiga's 1385 marriage to Władysław Jagiełło, the Grand Duke of Lithuania, led to Poland's strategic alliance with that powerful country. Following his wife's death, Jagiełło ruled both Poland and Lithuania for just shy of half a century, establishing a dynasty that would remain in power until 1572. The united countries defeated the Teutonic Knights at the Battle of Grunwald in 1410, halfway between Warsaw and the Lithuanian border, and repelled Germanic eastward expansion. The Thirteen Years' War yielded great benefits for Poland: the transformation of Danzig (Gdańsk) into an independent city-state under the protection of the Polish crown and the capture of other Knights' territories.

Polish nobles saw their political might expand in the early Renaissance with the king's 'rule of the nobility', which granted exclusive right to enact legislation to nobles in the parliament, or Sejm. The 1500s saw prosperity, power and cultural and scientific achievement for the Polish-Lithuanian Commonwealth. Just before his death in 1543 Mikołaj Kopernik (Nicolaus Copernicus), born in Toruń and a graduate of the Jagiellonian University in Kraków, published his groundbreaking treatise, *De Revolutionibus Orbium Coeliestium*, which stated that the sun and not the earth is the centre of the universe. Although the Reformation and Lutherism had an impact on Poland, the country largely avoided the devastating religious wars that raged elsewhere in Europe.

Monument to the Battle of Grunwald

The Sejm moved to Warsaw in 1529, and the death of the last ruler of the Jagiellonian dynasty, Zygmunt August, led to the creation of a Republic of Nobles and an elective monarchy that would serve it. Warsaw, better located in the centre of the country, became the official capital in 1596. King Zygmunt Waza (Sigismund Vasa) moved there from Kraków in 1609.

Swedish Dynasty

Three successive elected kings emerged from the Swedish Waza dynasty. Sweden had become the strongest military power in Europe after the Thirty Years' War and in the mid-17th century the country set its expansionist sights on Poland. The Swedes invaded Poland in 1648, an event labelled the Swedish Deluge in Polish history books. The devastating war lasted five years, during which time Sweden was able to capture most of Poland. The war and the disastrous effects of the plague decimated the population of Poland, reducing it to just 4 million, roughly half its total in the early 17th century.

Remarkably, Poland retained enough military might to repel the Ottoman Turks in their advance through the Balkans. The military leader Jan Sobieski defeated Turkish troops at the Battle of Chocim in 1673, and Sobieski would later be credited with saving Vienna from Turkish forces (and thwarting the Ottoman Empire's designs on Western Europe). Sobieski was elected king of Poland in 1674, but his attention to battles against the Turks at the expense of domestic affairs did not bode well for him and Poland.

Decline and Partitioning

At the start of the 18th century, Poland entered a prolonged period of decline, marked by financial ruin, a debilitated army, and a series of ineffectual kings. Poland was transformed into a client state of the Russians, and then lost much of its western territory to the Prussians during the Silesian Wars that ended in 1763. The following year Stanisław August Poniatowski was elected the last king of the Polish-Lithuanian Commonwealth, and Poland soon faced one of its most humiliating episodes.

The powerful Prussians came up with a plan to partition Poland, which gained the support of the Russians. The imposed treaty in 1772 robbed Poland of nearly a third of its lands. Yet Poniatowski recovered to preside over a reform movement that precipitated the creation of the 1791 Constitution, which restored the hereditary monarchy and overhauled Poland's political system. The liberal constitution, the oldest in the modern world after that of the United States, provided for the separation of powers among legislative, judicial and executive branches of the government.

None of these reforms pleased the Russians and Prussians, who continued to covet Polish territory. Russia invaded Poland and in 1792–3 it, along with Prussia, imposed a second partition of Poland, annulling the constitution and essentially divvying up the country between them. Tadeusz Kościuszko, a hero of the American War of Independence, led a military insurrection in 1794, defeating the Russians with a mostly peasant army. The uprising was quashed, however, and in 1795, Poniatowski was forced to abdicate. A third partition crushed Poland and placed the country under the control of Austria, Prussia and Russia. Poland ceased to exist for the next 123 years. Warsaw went to Prussia, Kraków to the mighty Austrian empire.

In desperation, Poland looked to Napoleon Bonaparte and Revolutionary France for assistance against its oppressors. Napoleon defeated the Prussian army in several key battles and established a semi-independent Duchy of Warsaw from 1807 to 1815. Napoleon gained an ally in Józef Poniatowski, a heralded military leader and the nephew of the last king. The 1812 Polish War re-established the Poland–Lithuania border, but Napoleon's troops were crushed as they advanced on Moscow. Napoleon suffered a great defeat, but his ally Poniatowski refused to surrender, preferring to sacrifice himself and his troops. The suicidal mission became an important rallying cry for Poles during the remainder of the 19th century.

The Congress of Vienna of 1815, which aimed to reorganise Europe after the Napoleonic Wars, did not re-establish an independent Poland. Rather, it re-partitioned the country, placing the Duchy of Warsaw under the control of the Russian tsar.

For three decades, Kraków existed as an independent city-state, though it was incorporated into the Austrian partition in 1846.

The former Duchy of Warsaw, called the Congress Kingdom, enjoyed some autonomy and prosperity in the early 19th century. Poles launched a series of armed insurrections against its occupiers in 1830 and, after defeat, again in 1846 and 1863. The last rebellion counted on support from England and France that never arrived. Many Poles, fearful that an independent Poland would never again be realised, emigrated to France and then the United States during this period. Those who remained focused on preserving Polish language and culture, if not the Polish state.

The Aftermath of World War I

The next pivotal episode in Polish history coincided with the end of World War I and the defeat of the Russians, Germans and Austrians. The partition of Poland collapsed in 1918,

The Cossack massacre during the January Uprising, 1863

and Poland's bid for independence won the support of both American president Woodrow Wilson and the Bolshevik government in Russia. The Polish war hero Józef Piłsudski (1867–1935), released from a German prison, took control of Poland. In 1920, the Soviets invaded, but Piłsudski and his troops managed to stop the advance at the Vistula and went on to occupy parts of Ukraine and Lithuania.

In 1926, Piłsudski engineered a military coup and seized control under the Sanacja, or senate, government that would rule until the start of World War II. By 1933, Poland was sandwiched between two dictatorships: Stalin in Russia on the eastern border, and Hitler in Nazi Germany to the west. Both fixed their eyes on occupying Poland, and they signed the ruthless Nazi–Soviet Pact on 23 August 1939, which stated that either would be free to pursue expansionist acts without the interference of the other. In the agreement was a secret clause providing for the eventual full partition of Poland between Germany and Russia – even though Poland had signed 10-year non-aggression pacts with both.

Nazi Invasion, World War II and the Holocaust

On 1 September 1939, the Nazis invaded Poland. The annexation of Danzig (modern day Gdańsk) marked the official start of World War II. Soon after, German forces launched an occupation of Kraków, where they based their governing body, and laid siege to Warsaw. The Soviets invaded Poland less than two weeks later on 17 September, following the terms of the pact signed with Germany.

The Nazis initiated a ruthless campaign in 1940, rounding up intellectuals, Jews and others, executing some in the streets and deporting others to concentration camps in the occupied territory. Craftsmen and labourers were deported to do forced labour in the Reich. Artists, scientists and priests were taken into 'protective custody', which was often a synonym for concentration camps. The Germans constructed walled Jewish ghettoes in Warsaw and Kraków. At death camps such as Auschwitz (see page 60), near Kraków, the Nazis eventually murdered millions of Poles, as well as other prisoners from across Europe. The Soviets themselves imprisoned some 1.5 million Poles in labour camps of their own and eliminated potential 'troublemakers' through actions like the Katyn massacre in 1940, in which more than 20,000 Polish military officers and civilians were summarily executed.

From 1941–5 Poland was under Nazi occupation, and the country became the focus of Hitler's campaign to exterminate

Hitler's bunker, known as 'the Lair', at Kętrzyn

Jews and non-Aryans. Hitler invaded the Soviet Union in 1941, an act that drew the Soviets and Poles together in a shaky alliance.

A heroic uprising in 1943, led by poorly armed Jews in the Warsaw ghetto, lasted a month until Nazi reinforcements annihilated it and reported back to Germany that 'Warsaw's Jewish quarter has ceased to exist'. The following year, Poland's Home Army initiated a surprise attack against the occupying Nazis in Warsaw, and awaited assistance from the Soviet Red Army, perched on the outskirts of the capital. The military support never came, and as his troops left the city after quashing the insurgency, Hitler ordered them to raze Warsaw building by building and thereby annihilate important monuments of Polish culture. When the Soviets entered the city, they found it reduced to rubble and ashes.

World War II was more devastating for Poland than any other country. Six million Poles lost their lives during World War II, and the Jewish population was reduced from three million to just a couple of thousand. Poland lost a significant amount of territory after new borders were drawn up in the Yalta Agreement of February 1945, including the eastern regions around Wilno (Vilnius) and Lwów (Lvov). The Polish borders shifted west a couple of hundred kilometres, incorporating ancient parts of Silesia such as Wrocław, the pre-war German city of Breslau. Poland also regained Danzig, not a part of Poland since its seizure by the Teutonic Knights. The city reverted to its original Polish name, Gdańsk.

Communism and Soviet Domination

In the aftermath of the war, Poland was Sovietised, with the installation of a Soviet-friendly communist regime, the nationalisation of businesses, confiscation of church property, and forced exile of political and religious leaders. With Soviet aid, a rebuilding programme was initiated, an effort that reconstructed the Old Towns of Warsaw and Gdańsk, among others, in costly and meticulous efforts based on paintings, photographs and architectural drawings. The Soviet Union signalled its domination over Poland with the 1955 'gift' of the Palace of Culture and Science in Warsaw, a towering skyscraper that would become a hated symbol of foreign influence.

Many Poles, especially among the intellectual and professional classes, opposed Soviet influence and Communist rule, and in 1956 the regime faced its first real test. Worker strikes and protests erupted in Poznań, and spread into armed confrontations in

Monument to the Warsaw Uprising, Warsaw

the streets. Security forces opened fire on rioters and killed scores of people, including a 13 year-old boy. A weakened and suddenly unstable Communist Party installed former First Secretary Gomułka as leader without consulting Moscow, an event that prompted Soviet, East German and Czech troops to mass on the Polish borders. A similar uprising occurred in Hungary the same year, and the Soviets invaded to quickly crush it.

But the episode in Poland, known as the Polish October, exposed cracks in the Communist regime, and served as the impetus for a slight relaxation of censorship, religious repression and economic controls. Reforms stalled, however, and the following decade saw a return to strict Soviet doctrine. The 1970s were marked by inflation and the emphatic suppression of strikes and protests. Living standards dropped dramatically, and the Soviet Union was forced to prop up the Polish economy.

Pope John Paul II and Solidarity

In 1978, the Polish Cardinal and Archbishop of Kraków Karol Wojtyła was elected Pope; he took the name John Paul II. A staunch opponent of the Communist regime, Wojtyła returned to Poland from Rome in 1979 as Pope and drew great, joyful crowds at every stop. The following year, unrest grew among workers after massive increases in food prices. Lech Wałęsa, a shipyard electrician, led strikes in Gdańsk. The size and vehemence of their protests, which spread countrywide, forced the government to negotiate with the Solidarność (Solidarity) trade union, granting its workers' demands and allowing free trade unions limited autonomy to oversee their industries. With hindsight, Solidarity was

Catholic Resistance

The Roman Catholic Church was one of the few institutions that retained a level of independence in Communist Poland, a fact that led to Stalin's celebrated remark comparing imposing Communism on the Poles to putting a saddle on a cow. The Communists did their best however, regarding the Church as a reactionary relic of the pre-war system. Repression was severe: priests and laymen alike were openly attacked and constantly threatened with arrest by the government, and by 1950 the financial assets of the Church had been confiscated. In 1953, one of the heroes of this frightening era, Cardinal Stefan Wyszyński, the primate of Poland, was arrested for his anti-state attitudes. He was exiled to a monastery where he was held prisoner for three years.

critical in establishing the foundations for opposition to Communist rule across Central and Eastern Europe.

General Wojciech Jaruzelski adopted a hard line and declared martial law in December 1981 in response to continued strikes across Poland. He initiated a military takeover of the Communist Party, and the government arrested thousands of Solidarity activists and sympathisers, banned the trade union and suspended civil rights. Two years later, the regime lifted martial law after the Pope John Paul's second visit to Poland, and Lech Wałęsa won the Nobel Peace Prize in 1983, familiarising the world with the struggles of Polish workers.

Palace of Culture, Warsaw

The government's resolve did not waver, however. In 1984, the Polish secret police murdered Father Jerzy Popiełuszko, an outspoken supporter of Solidarność.

The mid-1980s witnessed a gradual programme of liberalisation in Poland on the heels of Mikhail Gorbachev's perestroika and glasnost in the Soviet Union, the promises of greater openness and economic freedoms. The economic crisis in Poland persisted, though, and mass strikes were staged, even as Gorbachev visited Poland. In 1989, talks established the basis for limited power sharing between the Communist Party and Solidarity.

Polish Parliament in session

The End of Communist Rule

Desperate austerity measures failed to jump-start the economy. In semi-free elections, Solidarity was the overwhelming victor, and the Communist regime collapsed. On 9 December 1990, Poles made Lech Wałęsa the first popularly elected president in post-World War II Poland. In 1991, Wałęsa met the Pope in the Vatican. That same year, the Warsaw Pact was dissolved.

Poland's road to capitalism and democracy has been a complicated one. Wałęsa fell out of favour with Poles and was defeated in the 1995 elections. But by that time, the country had joined the World Trade Organization, and the EU had agreed to open negotiations to admit Poland.

Poland joined NATO in 1999 and the EU five years later. Huge crowds turned out for every one of John Paul II's many visits to his homeland up to and including his last visit in 2002, and his death in 2005 was widely mourned; both signs that Poland's committed Catholics and fervent patriots had survived Communism with their faith and pride intact. The country was rocked in April 2010, when the serving president Lech Kaczyński and his wife, former president Ryszard Kaczorowski and many important people in Polish politics, business and the military, were among the 96 passengers on board who all died in a plane crash near Smolensk. They were on their way to mark the 70th anniversary of the massacre at Katyn. The following year Poland assumed presidency of the European Union for the first time.

Historical Landmarks

966 The founding of Poland.

992 Bolesław I Chrobry (the Brave) is crowned first king of Poland.

1309 The Teutonic Order rules over a large territory along the Eastern Baltic Sea, including Gdańsk.

1325 Polish-Lithuanian alliance is formed against the Teutonic Knights.

1333 Kazimierz III Wielki (Casimir the Great) doubles the size of his realm, expanding to the east and transforming Poland into a multinational state.

1364 Founding of Kraków University.

1386 Founding of the Jagiellonian dynasty.

1410 Teutonic Knights are defeated at the Battle of Grunwald; Poland becomes a more powerful, unified realm.

1543 Nicolaus Copernicus publishes *De Revolutionibus Orbium Coelestium*.

1569 Poland and Lithuania are united into a single Commonwealth.

1655–60 Sweden invades Poland.

1673 Jan Sobieski defeats the Turks at the Battle of Chocim.

1772, 93, 95 Partitions divide Poland among Prussia, Austria and Russia.

1918 Independent Polish state created after the end of World War I.

1939 German troops invade Poland, triggering World War II.

1943 Warsaw Ghetto Uprising.

1944 Warsaw Uprising by Polish Home Army; city is razed by the Nazis.

1945 After the end of World War II, new borders are established by the victorious Allies. The Communists take power.

1956 Troops crush anti-government riots in Poznań.

1981 Martial law is proclaimed after disturbances spearheaded by the trade union Solidarity (Solidarność), led by Lech Wałęsa.

1989 Talks between Solidarity, the Communists and Catholic Church.

1990 Lech Wałęsa wins presidential election.

1999 Poland becomes a member of NATO.

2004 Poland joins the European Union (EU).

2005 Polish-born Pope John Paul II dies.

2010 President Lech Kaczyński among 96 dead in Smolensk plane crash.

2011 Poland assumes rotating presidency of the EU for the first time.

WHERE TO GO

Poland, bordering the Baltic Sea to the north, Germany to the west, the Czech Republic and Slovakia to the south, and Ukraine, Belarus, Lithuania and Russia to the east, is large and predominantly rural. The main points of interest for first-time visitors are the principal cities, beginning with Kraków, Warsaw and Gdańsk – whose old towns certainly rank among the finest of Central Europe, or Europe, for that matter – and smaller, well-preserved towns that are rich in history, architecture and Polish character. It is also a place to see great castles, memorials of Jewish culture that mark unspeakable tragedy, and churches and synagogues that are sites of important Catholic and Jewish pilgrimage.

It's easy and inexpensive to get around Poland by train, probably the preferred method of navigating the country. Exploring the Polish countryside, which seems several decades, if not more, behind the cities, requires either a lot of time and patience, or a car. And even one's personal transport can be sometimes be slow-going, as the Polish road system has lagged behind its speedy development in other areas, although new cross-country highways are making a big difference. For visitors with plenty of time, the mountains, sea and lake districts have much to offer, but this guide deals primarily with the major Polish cities and towns.

Because Kraków is the country's most popular tourist destination, this section begins there, in southeast Poland. Just beyond Kraków, reached in easy day trips, are the fantastic 700-year-old Wieliczka salt mines and the horrendous physical legacy of the Nazi concentration camps of Auschwitz. In southern Poland, along the Slovakian border, are the Tatra Mountains and the delightful ski resort town of Zakopane.

St Mary's Basilica on Kraków's Rynek Główny
(Main Market Square)

Adolf Hitler Platz

When Kraków was occupied by the Nazis, the Main Market Square was renamed Adolf Hitler Platz.

To the southeast of the country, between Kraków and Ukraine, is the 16th-century Renaissance town Zamość. Almost in the exact geographical centre of Poland is the present-day capital and commercial centre, Warsaw. Nearby is Łódź, Poland's second city. In north and northwest Poland are Gdańsk on the Baltic Sea, and nearby Malbork Castle, the most splendid fortification in Poland and the largest brick castle in the world. Toruń was the birthplace of the great Polish astronomer Copernicus, while Poznań is one of the most ancient centres in Poland and today one of its most dynamic cities.

KRAKÓW

Elegant **Kraków** ❶, the former royal capital of Poland, is one of the finest old cities in Europe. More than a thousand years old, and the country's capital for half that time, Kraków is Poland's third-largest city, with 750,000 residents, plus some 100,000 students. It is also considered the heart and soul of Poland, home to many of its greatest artists, writers, musicians, filmmakers and one of the world's oldest universities. It is one of the few major towns in Poland not devastated by the world wars of the 20th century, and its miraculously preserved medieval market square and castle hill make it Poland's most seductive city.

Though awe-inspiring churches, monuments and museums line its ancient streets, and the historic royal castle overlooks the Old Town from a hilltop, Kraków is one of Poland's liveliest and hippest cities. It abounds with young, fashionable café-hoppers. Kraków's roster of bars and cafés, many of them idiosyncratic places in underground cellars, are among the city's undeniable highlights. Almost everything of interest in Kraków is easily managed on foot, with the possible exception of Kazimierz, the old Jewish quarter that lies just south of the Old Town. Though a visitor could rush through Kraków and 'see' its Old Town and Wawel Hill in a couple of days, one would miss out on much of the alluring character of the city, which is best savoured over several days or a week.

Main Market Square and Old Town

Kraków's layout dates from 1257 and remains almost unchanged to this day. The streets are lined with historic townhouses, fine churches and delightful small shops. The whole of the largely pedestrianised Old Town (Stare Miasto) is encircled by the **Planty**, a ring of relaxing parklands where massive fortifications and a wide moat once protected the city. The best place to begin to get to know Kraków is Europe's largest medieval Market Square, **Rynek Główny** , at the heart of the Old Town. The spectacular square pulsates with youthful energy at all hours, and

Rynek Główny (Main Market Square)

its pavement cafés are fine places to enjoy the views of the square, Kraków's beautiful people, its traditional horse-drawn carriages and its huge flock of pigeons. Many of the houses that line the square have Neo-Classical façades, though they are considerably older than that, and are full of interesting architectural details.

At the centre of the square is the **Cloth Hall** (Sukiennice), built in the 14th century and reconstructed after a fire in 1555 in the Renaissance style (the arcades were added in the 19th century). The building once housed the richest of Kraków's cloth merchants, and today its ground-floor stalls are occupied by privileged sellers of amber jewellery, religious artefacts, art and souvenirs targeting Kraków's year-round tourist trade. Indeed, the entire market square was once populated with merchants of all kinds, though today the only ones permitted are flower sellers and artists (as well as booths set up for special fairs).

Next to the Cloth Hall is the 15th-century **Town Hall Tower**; the rest of the Town Hall was demolished in the early 19th century. Southeast of it is tiny **St Adalbert's Church** (Kościół Św. Wojciecha). Intriguingly, the copper-domed 11th-century church is a few steps down, showing the original level of the square. The branch of the **Kraków Historical Museum** (Rynek Główny 35; most of the building is closed for renovation until 2014) in the former Krzysztofory Palace, dates back to the Middle

St Mary's Trumpeter

Every hour, a trumpeter appears in the tallest tower of St Mary's Basilica to play the Hejnał Mariacki, a call to arms that began as a warning of the advancing Tartar army in 1241. The tradition has been continued down the centuries ever since. The bugle call ends mid-bar, a symbol of the story that the lone watchman was felled by an arrow as he warned the city. Watch the trumpeter from the passageway just south of the church; at the end of the piece, he waves to those gathered below.

Ages and is devoted to displays showing the development of the city, as well as being home to the wonderful traditional exhibition of Christmas cribs every December.

Under the Cloth Hall's arches

St Mary's Basilica

On the eastern side of the square, just beyond a statue of the 19th-century Romantic poet Adam Mickiewicz – a hangout for local youths and backpackers from around the globe – is **St Mary's Basilica** **B** (Kościół Mariacki; Mon–Sat 11.30am–6pm, Sun 2–6pm; charge). Its asymmetrical towers are one of Kraków's most celebrated images and the hejnał, or bugle call sounds hourly from the tallest tower, one of Poland's iconic sounds. A church was founded on this spot in 1221–2, and it faced east, as was the custom of the day. St Mary's, built on the original foundations in the 14th century, also sits at an angle to the square.

The main entrance, a Baroque porch façade, is used only by those attending Mass. Tourists are asked to enter through the side door, through Plac Mariacki off Rynek Główny. Inside is a stunning kaleidoscope of ornamentation and colour, with extraordinary wall paintings by Jan Matejko in blue, green and pink. The ceiling of the main nave is painted a bold blue with gold stars. The highlight, set beneath five tall columns of stained-glass windows, is the sumptuous altarpiece, a master-work of Polish Gothic that took the 15th-century German mas-ter carver Veit Stoss (Wit Stwosz) 12 years to create in linden wood. The powerful triptych shows the Dormition of the Virgin Mary, flanked by scenes of the life of Christ and the Virgin. Over the central nave is a massive crucifix; at the rear of the church, behind the organ loft are fine examples of Art Nouveau stained glass, the work of Kraków's Stanisław Wyspiański.

The little courtyard south of St Mary's leads to **St Barbara's Church** (Kościół Św. Barbary) and a passageway onto **Little Market Square** (Mały Rynek), where colourful façades line what was once the marketplace of meat, fish and poultry vendors (whose wares were moved from the Main Market Square due to their unpleasant odours).

Leading north off the Main Market Square is ul. Floriańska, a busy pedestrian-only street full of shops, restaurants and cafés. On the eastern side is the **Jan Matejko House** (Dom Jana Matejki; Tue–Sat 10am–6pm, Sun 10am–4pm; charge), the home where the influential 19th-century Polish artist was born, worked and died. It includes memorabilia and a number of paintings from his personal collection, and much of the house stands as the artist left it upon his death in 1893, though

Inside St Mary's Basilica

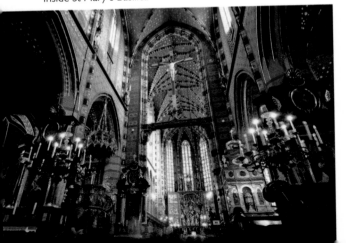

it was restored in 2009 to include multimedia installations illuminating his life story and newly uncovered wall paintings. At the end of the street, and the edge of the Old Town, is **Florian's Gate** C (Brama Floriańska), one of the original seven gates in the city's fortified walls. Built early in the 14th century, it is the only one to have survived 19th-century modernisation plans. An outdoor art market takes place here daily, and pictures executed in every conceivable style blanket the stone walls. The view down Floriańska towards the spire of St Mary's is one of the most priceless in Kraków.

Just beyond the gate is the **Barbican** D (Barbakan; Apr–Oct daily 10.30am–6pm; charge), a circular brick bastion built at the end of the 15th century and one of the few remaining structures of the medieval fortifications. It was originally connected to the Floriańska Gate over a moat. Nearby are two buildings of significance. On the edge of the Planty to the southeast is the **Church of the Holy Cross** (Kościół Św. Krzyża; pl. Św. Ducha), a small 15th-century church with splendid Gothic vaulting; almost next to it is the eclectic **Słowacki Theatre** (Teatr im. Juliusza Słowackiego; pl. Św. Ducha 1), a bright yellow-and-green-roofed structure built in 1893 and modelled after the Paris Opera House. Don't miss the curious laughing gargoyles on the rooftop.

The Czartoryski and Wyspiański Museums

At the top of ul. Św. Jana, the street running parallel to and to the west of Floriańska, is one of the Old Town's highlights – the **Czartoryski Museum** E (Muzeum Czartoryskich). The main building of the museum is closed for restoration until 2013, when visitors will once again be able to see a fine collection made by this prominent Kraków family in the palace that was once their home. Until it re-opens, some of the museum's most popular treasures, such as Leonardo da Vinci's *Lady with an Ermine* and Rembrandt's *Landscape with the Good*

Samaritan, will be displayed at the Szołayski House branch of the **National Museum in Kraków** (Muzeum Stanisława Wyspiańskiego w Kamienicy Szołayskich, ul. Szczepańska 11; Tue–Sat 10am–6pm, Sun 10am–4pm, Mon closed; charge). See the museums' websites (www.muzeum.krakow.pl; www.fundacja-czartoryskich.krakow.pl) for details. Meanwhile, the Czartoryski's Ancient Art Gallery, with splendid examples from works from Greece, Eturia, Egypt and Rome, has reopened in the Arsenal building across the street from the main building (Galerii Sztuki Starożytnej w Arsenale Książąt Czartoryskich; Tue–Sun 10am–4pm; charge).

Apart from hosting the Czartoryski treasures while their place is being modernised, the **Stanisław Wyspiański Museum** (Muzeum Stanisław a Wyspiańskiego; May–Oct Wed, Sat 10am–7pm, Thur–Fri 10am–4pm, Sun 10am–3pm;

Czartoryski Museum, Rembrandt's *Landscape with the Good Samaritan*

Nov–Apr Wed–Thur, Sat–Sun 10am–3pm, Fri 10am–6pm; charge) features the art, design and writings of the Kraków artist. Wyspiański is perhaps best known for his stained glass and decorative frescoes (as seen in St Francis' Basilica; see page 43), but he was also a poet, designer and dramatist. This branch of the National Museum, in a 17th-century house, holds a large collection of Wyspiański's works, including architectural designs for civic buildings, stained-glass windows for churches, stage sets, portraits and landscapes.

Jagiellonian University

The area south and west of the main market square is home to the famed **Jagiellonian University**, the oldest university in Poland and one of the oldest in Europe, and several fine churches. Take any of the streets heading west from the square, such as Św. Anny. Enter a small door beneath the Flemish-style roof to the **Collegium Maius** ❺, the oldest building of the university and a beautiful 15th-century Gothic structure with an arcaded central courtyard. Notice the fanciful drainage pipe heads, of medieval dragons and the like, on the rooftop. King Kazimierz established the university in 1364, but its golden age dates to the period of the reign of King Jagiełło, for whom it is named. Copernicus allegedly studied here in the 15th century.

Here you will find the **Jagiellonian University Museum** (Muzeum Uniwersytetu Jagiellońskiego; Apr–Oct Mon, Wed, Fri 10am–3pm, Tue, Thur 10am–6pm, Sat 10am–2pm, Sun closed; Nov–Mar Mon, Wed, Fri 10am–3pm, Tue 10am–4pm, Sat 10am–2pm, Sun, Thur closed; charge; times vary for English language tours; advance booking recommended, tel: 012 663 15 21). On the guided visit through the ornate academic halls, the treasury, library and professors' dining hall – you can see several objects related to the university's most famous collegian and his theory that revolutionised our notion of the universe, including astronomical instruments,

A tour group at Collegium Maius

a registrar's book signed 'Mikołaj Kopernik', and a very rare globe, dating back to 1520, with the earliest known depiction of the Americas. Pope John Paul II was once an undergraduate at this university, and Poland's most recent Nobel Prize winner for literature, the late Wisława Szymborska, donated her medal and a good portion of the prize to the museum.

Old Town Churches

The streets near here are always filled with students – Kraków has nearly 100,000 students attending the university's 12 colleges and academic institutes. Around the corner from the Collegium Maius is **St Anne's Church** (Kościół Św. Anny; ul. Św. Anny 11), linked to the university and a favourite location for students getting married. The 17th-century interior is a superb example of airy Polish Baroque, with a high dome, spectacular stucco work and wall murals. Facing the Planty is the **Collegium Novum**, a late 19th-century neo-Gothic building decorated with the crests of the university and its most celebrated benefactors. When Hitler's troops invaded Kraków in 1939, they stormed this hall and arrested nearly 200 professors and academics, and hauled them off to concentration camps.

On ul. Franciszkańska, directly south of the market square, is the unmissable **St Francis' Basilica** Ⓖ (Kościół Św. Franciszka z Asyżu; pl. Wszystkich Świętych), dating from 1269. The gutted interior was rebuilt in the 19th century after the last of four disastrous fires. Relatively unassuming from the exterior, the exuberant interior is a stunning assembly of brilliant stained glass and colourful wall paintings in floral and geometric motifs. At the rear above the organ loft is a remarkable Art Nouveau stained-glass window designed by the local artist Stanisław Wyspiański, a disciple of Jan Matejko, in 1900. The large 'Act of Creation' depicts God in wild streaks of colour. Wyspiański reportedly based God's face on the countenance of a beggar. The stained-glass windows behind the altar, also by Wyspiański, depict the Blessed Salomea to the left and St Francis to the right. To the right of the altar is a passage to the Gothic cloister with its 15th-century frescoes and portraits of the bishops of Kraków. The painting at the end of the hall is of the 'lady who stopped the fire,' a reference to the great fire of 1850 that was miraculously snuffed out at that very wall of the Franciscan church.

East of here the street changes name in honour of another religious order and its 13th-century church, the **Dominican Church and Monastery** (Kościół Dominikanów; ul. Stolarska 12). It too suffered from fire damage, and today is notable for its neo-Gothic chapels and original 15th-century portal. The monastery has serene Gothic cloisters.

Heading south towards Wawel Hill, along ul. Grodzka, is **SS Peter and**

City of churches

Kraków is said to have in excess of 125 churches – 60 of them in the Old Town alone.

Sculptures in front of SS Peter and Paul's Church

Paul's Church �H (Kościół Św. Piotra i Św. Pawła; ul. Grodzka 54), recognised by its large dome and long row of stately statues of the Twelve Apostles out front. The oldest Baroque building in Kraków, the basilica was founded by the Jesuits in the early 1600s. The rather austere late-Renaissance interior has recently been renovated.

The small Romanesque church next door is **St Andrew's** (Kościół Św. Andrzeja; ul. Grodzka 56), dating from the 11th century and one of the oldest churches in Kraków. Its colourful history includes a stint as a hiding place and fortress for Poles battling invading Tartars in 1241.

Across the square facing those two churches, turn down ul. Kanonicza, one of Kraków's oldest and most attractive streets. On the way to Wawel Hill, at ul. Kanonicza 9, is the house where Stanisław Wyspiański lived and worked in the early 20th century.

Down the street, at ul. Kanonicza 19, is the **Archdiocesan Museum** 🟙 (Muzeum Archidiecezjalne; ul. Kanonicza 19;

Tue–Fri 10am–4pm, Sat–Sun 10am–3pm; charge), where Pope John Paul II lived on two occasions, first as a young priest and then as Bishop of Kraków. The neighbouring 14th-century houses now contain a small museum of notable 13th- to 20th-century religious art, including a collection of Gothic sculptures of the Madonna and child, and artefacts belonging to the Pope, including the room where he lived (with his desk, bed and two pairs of skis), photographs, and ornate gifts from heads of state and religious leaders.

The other buildings on ul. Kanonicza are also worth a closer look, as many are former palaces with a range of architectural features, including Gothic, Renaissance and Baroque. Continuing along ul. Kanonicza, past the exclusive Hotel Copernicus, leads you towards Wawel Hill.

Wawel Hill

A castle or royal palace has existed on Wawel Hill overlooking the Old Town of Kraków since the 9th century, though the area may have been inhabited as early as the Paleolithic Age. The first kings of Poland maintained a royal residence here from the 10th century until King Zygmunt Waza (Sigismund Vasa) moved the royal seat to Warsaw in 1596. Over the centuries the castle was repeatedly destroyed by invaders and war, ultimately transformed into the complex that today is a mix of Gothic, Renaissance, Baroque and neo-Classical architecture.

Ticket tips

Separate tickets are needed for the cathedral and castle complexes. Guided group visits are available at the main box office past the cathedral (there are two other box offices, including one on the path on the way up the hill). The various component parts of Wawel have different opening hours, so be sure to check them before visiting. For the latest information, check the official Wawel website at www.wawel.krakow.pl.

Wawel, a symbol of the Polish nation, is a great source of national pride to Poles, and it is a popular place of spiritual pilgrimage. The most popular sites to visit are the royal castle and chambers, treasury and armoury, the cathedral and royal tombs, and Sigismund stairs to the bell tower. Expect crowds and large tour groups, especially in summer, and allow at least half a day for a visit and a day for a full visit.

The Cathedral

The Gothic edifice of **Wawel Cathedral** ❶ (Katedra; Apr–Sept Mon-Sat 9am–5pm, Sun 12.30pm–5pm; Oct–Mar Mon–Sat 9am–4pm, Sun 12.30pm–4pm Cathedral Museum closed Sun; Cathedral free; charge only for the crypt, bell tower and Cathedral Museum) – the third cathedral built on this site – was begun in 1320, some three centuries after the first. The site of half a millennium of royal coronations and burials, it

Inside Wawel Cathedral

is the final resting place of nearly all the kings of Poland. The entrance is marked by a set of very large bones – those of a prehistoric woolly rhinoceros – that were found on the site and are said to protect the cathedral and all Kraków against those who would attempt to harm the city.

At the centre of the nave is an ornate **shrine to St Stanislaus** (św Stanisław), the 13th-century bishop of Kraków who was martyred by the Polish king Bolesław in 1079. The saint's body was dismembered but, according to legend, it became whole again – a sign taken as a portent that a divided Poland, partitioned by Germany, Russia and Austria, would also reunify itself. The cathedral witnessed the coronation of 32 kings, each of whom knelt before the shrine and asked St Stanislaus for forgiveness. Of particular interest among the various tombs, altars and chapels is the highly ornamented, Renaissance-style **Sigismund Chapel**, designed by the Italian architect Bartolomeo Berrecci (it's the one with the gleaming golden dome seen from outside). To the right of the entrance, the **Holy Cross Chapel** is a feast of extraordinary 14th-century Byzantine frescoes and the late 15th-century marble sarcophagus of King Casimir IV Jagiełło, which was carved in reddish marble by Veit Stoss.

The steep, wooden 14th-century stairs leading to the **Sigismund Belltower** are not for the claustrophobic or disabled, but for the athletically inclined. They are a fun climb up to see the revered Zygmunt bell, which dates to the mid-16th century and is the largest bell in Poland, requiring eight people to ring it. Krakovians say they can hear the bell from as far as 20km (12 miles) away when it is rung on major holidays.

Next to the altar is the tomb of Kazimierz the Great, the so-called 'Builder of Poland'. The sepulchres of the Sigismund kings, the beloved Queen Jadwiga and others lie in the main body of the cathedral, while below in the **Royal Crypts** are the tombs of 10 Polish kings and their families, as well as a handful of national military and literary heroes, including

Wawel Castle

Marshal Piłsudski, who has a small and decidedly atmospheric crypt all to himself. The entrance to the tombs is towards the back of the church, and the exit is onto the main castle courtyard.

Castle Highlights

Wawel Castle K, also an enduring symbol of Polish nationhood, was the royal residence until the capital moved to Warsaw in 1596. King Bolesław built the first and considerably smaller residence in the 11th century, but it became a grand, Gothic palace during the reign of Kazimierz the Great in the 14th century. A great fire razed it in 1499, and the elegant Renaissance palace that was rebuilt by King Zygmunt the Old is largely the structure one sees today. Swedes, Prussians and Austrians all overran and occupied the castle and its grounds at different times, and the last group of invaders destroyed churches and built military barracks, leaving the hill with an oddly empty square and large and plainer buildings to the west of the castle. The Polish government and people did not recover Wawel until the end of World War I in 1918, when the partition of Poland ended.

Visitor numbers on the hill are restricted, and entry to some of the sights is by timed ticket only. To reserve in advance tel: 012 422 51 55 ext. 291 or 012 422 16 97. Collect reserved tickets at the Tourist Service Office (Biuro Obsługi Turystów), inside the square near the entrance to the arcaded courtyard at least 20 minutes before the reserved time, or from the ticket offices at Herbowa Gate (Brama Herbowa) or Bernadyńska Gate. You can also reserve timed tickets at these ticket offices. See www.wawel.krakow.pl.

The **State Rooms** and **Royal Private Apartments** (Reprezentacyjne Komnaty Królewskie and Prywatne Apartamenty Królewskie; Apr–Oct Tue–Fri 9.30am–5pm, Sat–Sun 10am– 4pm, Mon closed; Nov–Mar Tue–Fri 9.30am–5pm, Sat 9.30am–4pm, Sun 10am–4pm, Royal Private Apartments closed Sun, both closed Mon all year; charge; State Rooms free Sun Nov–Mar; admission to Royal Private Apartments in groups of up to 10, guided tours only, fee includes guide service) are the largest and most interesting part of the castle. They have been restored to their original Renaissance style and furnished with Baroque and Renaissance furniture, much of which is not original to the castle but certainly representative of royal lifestyle. The most impressive and valuable items on display are the spectacular collection of 16th-century Flemish tapestries commissioned by King Sigismund. Only 136 of the original 364 tapestries (all ordered at the same time) survive, and not all are on view. The tapestries have a particularly peripatetic history. At various times, many were stolen and others taken out of the country for safekeeping. When World War II broke out, they were taken from Romania to France and England and finally Canada before being restored to Poland in the 1960s.

Also on view is a handsome collection of 17th-century Turkish tents in an exhibition of Oriental art.

The **Deputies Hall**, or Throne Room, is also called the 'Room of Heads', a name that is explained once you glance at the ceiling. It is studded with small carved wooden heads of some 30 citizens of Renaissance-period Kraków – ordinary folk, not just royalty, nobles and clergy as might be expected. Over the king's throne is a stunning Flemish tapestry. The **Senators'**

Room is tapestried wall-to-wall, with tapestries placed over the windows, reportedly so there would be no outside distractions during important Senate sessions. It is the only room where the original placement of tapestries is known.

The **Treasury and Armoury** (Skarbiec Koronny i Zbrojownia; Apr–Oct Mon 9.30am–1pm, Tue–Fri 9.30am–5pm, Sat–Sun 10am–5pm; Nov–Mar Tue–Sat 9.30am–4pm, closed Mon–Sun; charge, free Mon Apr–Oct), in vaulted Gothic rooms that were part of the 14th-century castle, house the royal collection of weaponry and spoils of war, including the 13th-century Szczerbiec, a Royal jagged sword used at all Polish coronations.

Lost Wawel is an exhibition, across the garden from the cathedral, housed within the former royal kitchens and coach house (Wawel Zaginiony; Apr–Oct Mon 9.30am–1pm, Tue–Fri 9.30am–5pm, Sat–Sun 10am–5pm; Nov–Mar Tue–Sat 9.30am–4pm, Sun 10am–4pm, closed Mon; charge, free Mon Apr–Oct Sun Nov–Mar) in which some fascinating archaeological and architectural remains are on display,

At the far end of the castle grounds, (walk towards the Baszta Sandomierska exit) you will find Wawel's **Dragon's Cave** (Smocza Jama; daily Apr, Sept, Oct 10am–5pm; May–June 10am–6pm; July–Aug 10am–7pm; Nov–Mar closed; charge), according to legend the home of a reclusive dragon, Smok Wawelski. From here you emerge on the banks of the Vistula River.

Kazimierz

Once the old Jewish district of Kraków, **Kazimierz** ❶ was originally built in 1335 as an independent, planned and walled town by the Polish king whose name it took. Jews, persecuted throughout Europe, were offered refuge all over Kraków, but King Jan Olbracht moved Kraków's entire Jewish population to Kazimierz at the end of the 15th century. Today the district is essentially a suburb within easy walking distance or a short tram or taxi ride from the Old Town.

Before the war, some 60,000 Jews lived in the Kraków area. Only a few thousand remained in 1945, and today there are reportedly as few as 200 here. After decades of neglect, having been robbed of its people and soul – although many of its buildings survived the war – Kazimierz is undergoing a revitalisation. Jewish foundations from around the world are funding the restoration of historic buildings, and Steven Spielberg brought new attention to Kazimierz with his Academy Award-winning 1994 film Schindler's List, though only a few scenes were filmed in the area. As visitors to Kraków discover Kazimierz, new hotels, cafés and restaurants are moving in, and there are signs that young Krakovians now see it as more than the devastating reminder of a tragic period in Polish history.

The easiest way to get to Kazimierz is to walk from the Old Town, but any tram or bus going from the Planty down ul. Stradomska or Starowiślna will have one or two stops in

A stylish Kazimierz café

Kazimierz, such as ul. Miodowa or Plac Wolnica. If walking from Wawel Hill, take ul. Stradomska (which becomes ul. Krakowska) south and turn left at ul. Józefa.

There are fewer and fewer dilapidated buildings now but still among the new businesses in the Jewish quarter you can see many signs of Jewish life in Kazimierz. Eight synagogues (of the 30 that once existed here) survived the war, of which a couple have been established as museums. Ul. Szeroka, which means Wide Street but is actually more of a square, was the heart of the district from the 15th century onwards. On the west side of the square is the **Remu'h Synagogue and Cemetery** (ul. Szeroka 40; Sun–Fri 9am–4pm; charge), a small 500-year-old synagogue that remains in use. The second-oldest in the

Remu'h Cemetery

district, it is perhaps the most important synagogue in the area today. Jews visit to touch the chair of the 16th-century Rabbi Moses Isserles, a great philosopher and lawyer, and a black feast calendar is one of the few surviving elements of the original synagogue. Much of the cemetery next door was destroyed by the Nazis, though several hundred gravestones, many of them 400 years old and buried by the Jews themselves to avoid desecration by invaders of the 18th century, were discovered during excavations after the war. The handful of tombs enclosed by a fence includes that of Rabbi Isserles, which is often covered with small stones, measures of respect left behind by Jewish visitors. Legend holds that the Nazis were in the process of levelling the rabbi's grave along with all the others when one of the workers was felled by a heart attack. The Wailing Wall at one end of the cemetery is made up of fragments of gravestones that were destroyed by the Germans.

Jewish culture

Now running for over 20 years, the annual Jewish Festival of Culture is a great way to discover both Kraków's Jewish past and the vibrant Jewish culture that remains in the city. Highlights of the 10-day festival include kosher cooking, Hassidic dancing and some of the best Klezmer music you'll hear. For more information, see www.jewishfestival.pl.

At the south end of ul. Szeroka is the **Old Synagogue** (ul. Szeroka 24; Apr– Oct Mon 10am–2pm, Tue–Sun 9am–5pm; Nov–Mar Tue–Wed, Sat–Sun 9am–4pm, Mon 10am–2pm, Fri 10am–5pm; charge, Mon free). Dating from the 15th century, it is the oldest surviving Jewish house of worship in Poland. Today it houses a museum of Jewish history and culture, with an ornate 16th-century wrought-iron bimah, or pulpit, in the centre of the main prayer hall. A monument in front of the museum marks the site where 30 Polish men and boys were executed by Nazis in 1943. A plaque marks the spot where Polish revolutionary Tadeusz Kościuszko rallied the Jews to join his fight for Polish independence in 1794.

One street to the west is the large **Isaac Synagogue** (ul. Kupa 18; Sun–Fri 9am–7pm; charge), a cavernous hall that was once the most beautiful of all the synagogues here, with opulent Baroque stucco decoration from the mid-17th century that was destroyed by the Nazis, though restoration work is under way. Today, at the end of the otherwise empty room, school groups and other visitors sit silently in front of televisions and watch a sombre documentary of Jewish life (The Memory of Polish Jews) set to plaintive music that evokes the

Holocaust. Next to the synagogue is an atmospheric, bohemian café, **Singer**, where some of the tables are old Singer sewing machine stands and which can be credited with inspiring many lace-strewn imitators in the area.

The **Jewish Cultural Centre** (ul. Rabina Meiselsa 17; Mon–Fri 10am–6pm, Sat–Sun 10am–2pm; www.judaica.pl) is located just west of pl. Nowy, the old Jewish marketplace. It has regular exhibitions and conferences aimed at preserving knowledge of Jewish culture. A superb photographic exhibition of Jewish heritage can be seen at the **Galicia Jewish Museum** (ul. Dajwór 18; daily 9am–7pm; charge; www.galiciajewishmuseum.org), which also runs a very full programme of cultural events and is a good place to begin to make sense of what you see in Kazimierz.

Western Kazimierz is the Catholic section of the planned town and is marked by three churches: **Corpus Christi Church** (Kościół Bozego Ciała; ul. Bozego Ciała 26), the Gothic **St Catherine's Church** (Kościół Św. Katarzyny; ul. Augustiańska 7) and the **Pauline Church** (Kościół Paulinów; ul. Skałeczna), known as 'the Church on the Rock.' Celebrated cultural figures, including Stanisław Wyspiański, are buried in the crypt of the latter, where it is also said that Kraków's St Adalbert was mutilated and then miraculously resurrected. On pl. Wolnica is the old town hall, which now houses an **Ethnographic Museum** (Muzeum Etnograficzne; pl. Wolnica 1; Tue–Wed, Fri–Sat 11am–7pm, Thur 11am–9pm, Sun 11am–3pm; charge, Sun free), said to be the largest in the country, with exhibits that depict the region's rural and folk traditions.

The **New Jewish Cemetery** (Nowy Cmentarz Żydowski; ul. Miodowa 55; Sun–Fri 9am–dusk), a short

In the ghetto

Jews in the war-time ghetto were required by the Nazis to: have a Star of David designating all businesses; carry Jewish identity cards at all times; and ride on the back half of trams, which were labelled Für Juden (for Jews).

walk northeast of ul. Szeroka, is a large, haunted-looking place of toppled gravestones with Yiddish insignias and lettering grown over by bright green moss. The cemetery was founded in 1800 and, though appearing wholly abandoned today, is the only current burial place for Jews in Kraków.

The actual ghetto where the Nazis forced the Jews to live between 1941 and 1943 is located across the river over Powstańców Śląskich bridge at the end of ul. Starowiślna, in the Podgórze district. Here you'll find another place of interest and pilgrimage, the **Museum of National Remembrance** (Muzeum Pamięci Narodowej; pl.

Commemorating Jewish history in the Galicia Museum

Bohaterów Getta 18; Apr–Oct Mon 10am–2pm, Tue–Sun 9.30am–5pm; Nov–Mar Mon 10am–2pm, Tue–Thur and Sat 9am–4pm, Fri 10am–5pm, closed Sun and first Tue of month Nov–Mar; charge, free Mon), better known as the Pharmacy Under the Eagle (Apteka pod Orłem). Now a small museum of Jewish life in the ghetto, it was once a pharmacy belonging to a Pole – the only Gentile whom the Germans allowed to live in the ghetto – who witnessed the murders of 1,000 Jews and tried to shelter and help as many as he could. Tadeusz Pankiewicz later was one of the critical witnesses at the Nuremberg trials. Nearby, off ul. Lwowska to the southwest of the pharmacy, is a still-standing section of the wall that the Nazis constructed around the

Photograph in the Museum of
National Remembrance

ghetto. If the top of the wall looks familiar, it is because Hitler's agents designed the wall to mimic the form of traditional Jewish gravestones, the message delivered a clear 'here is where you shall die'.

Across pl. Bohaterów Ghetta (Heros of the Ghetto Square) Oskar Schindler's former Emalia enamel factory is now home to a 'factory of memory', a powerful multimedia exhibition of the Nazi Occupation of 1939–45 (Fabryka Schindlera; ul. Lipowa 4; Apr–Oct Mon 10am–2pm, Tue–Sun 10am–8pm; Nov–Mar Mon 10am–2pm, Tue–Sun 10am–6pm, closed first Mon of every month; charge, Mon free; last admission 90 mins before closing; under-14s must be accompanied by their parents; www.mhk.pl to reserve advance tickets online). Next door, the former factory floor was transformed in 2011 into the **Museum of Contemporary Art in Kraków** (MOCAK, Muzeum Sztuki Współczesnej w Krakowie; Tue–Sun noon–8pm; charge, Tue free), which hosts temporary exhibitions of international art.

Most visitors to Kraków stick to the Old Town and Wawel Hill, and perhaps Kazimierz and separate trips to Auschwitz and the Wieliczka Salt Mines. If you have more time, though, just west of the Old Town is the **National Museum** (Muzeum Narodowe; al. 3 Maja 1; Tue–Fri 10am–6pm, Sun 10am–4pm, Mon closed; charge, Sun permanent collection free; www.muzeum.krakow.pl). The off-putting, Soviet-style architecture houses an important collection including 14th-century stained glass and decorative arts, furniture and vestments from Wawel, a wonderful collection of paintings, sculptures and other works by leading 20th-century

Polish artists and a wide array of military armaments and uniforms, of great interest to history enthusiasts. It also hosts most of the important touring exhibitions that come to Kraków.

Those interested in architecture and Oriental culture should visit **Manggha** (ul. Konopnickiej 26; Oct–June Tue–Sun 10am–6pm; July–Sept 10am–8pm, charge), across the river south of Wawel Hill and west of Kazimierz. The splendidly futuristic building, designed by the Japanese architect Arata Isozaki, and funded by one of Poland's most celebrated film directors Andrzej Wajda. Named for Feliks 'Manggha' Jasieński (1861-1929), a noted collector of Japanese art, it operates as a cultural centre hosting temporary exhibitions, mainly of Oriental art and its café is pleasant place to nibble on some sushi.

EXCURSIONS FROM KRAKÓW

Wieliczka Salt Mines

Wieliczka ❷ (ul. Daniłowicza 10, Wieliczka; daily for guided tours only; Apr–Oct 7.30am–7.30pm; Nov–Mar 8am–5pm;

Oskar Schindler

Immortalised first in Thomas Keneally's book *Schindler's Ark* and later in the Oscar-winning film *Schindler's List,* directed by Steven Spielberg, the enigmatic German businessman Oskar Schindler (1908–74) lived and worked in Kraków during World War II. He bought a bankrupt enamel factory in Podgórze and employed cheap Jewish labour, saving thousands of lives by bribing and hoodwinking scores of high-ranking Nazis throughout the war. His famous list dates from the summer of 1944, and was made up of 1,100 Jewish men, women and children destined for the gas chambers at Auschwitz whom he saved by sending to another factory he owned in what is now the Czech Republic. After his death Schindler was buried on Jerusalem's Mount Zion, recognised as one of the Righteous Among Nations.

charge; www.kopalnia.pl), a series of deep mines more than 700 years old located about 10km (6 miles) southeast of Kraków, makes for an extraordinary subterranean adventure. The mine reaches 327m (1,073ft) and nine levels underground. Visitors descend 378 steps down to the first level of 64m (210ft) and then pass through 2km (1.25 miles) of tunnels, visiting some 20 chambers and chapels carved out of salt by miners. The Baroque St Anthony Chapel dates to 1690–1710, but the largest and most astounding chapel is the **Chapel of the Blessed St Kinga**. Like the other chambers, everything in it is carved out of salt. Its chandeliers, altar and remarkable relief carving (with great perspective) of the Last Supper were created over a period of 70 years, and were begun, in the 19th century, by just three miners, who were obviously talented and dedicated sculptors (like all the chapels and chambers, this massive hall was carved in the miners' time off). Weddings are occasionally held in the St Kinga Chapel, as is Mass three times a year. Along the way in other chambers you'll also see green-salt statues of Copernicus and even, curiously, the Seven Dwarves.

Inside Wieliczka Salt Mine

Listed by UNESCO as a World Heritage Site, the mine was the property of the Polish Royal Family (for whom the salt, called 'grey gold', contributed one-third of the total royal wealth) until the 1772 partition of Poland, when it fell to the Austrians. Salt mining continued here until 1996, and today the mine is visited by tour groups and those seeking relief from respiratory ailments like asthma in the sanatorium 135m (450ft) below ground. During World War II, the Nazis used the tallest chamber (which measures 36m/118ft from floor to ceiling) as a secret factory for the manufacture of aircraft parts, staffed by Jewish prisoners. A few years back, a couple of thrillseekers pulled off a bungee jump and others conducted the first underground balloon flight, documented by the Guinness Book of World Records, in the same chamber. During July and August, a miners' orchestra plays in the lake chamber, treating visitors to a 170-year-old tradition, and the mine is a popular venue for jazz concerts and other special events.

At the end of the three-hour visit to the mine, you can visit the museum of mining equipment and geological specimens or stop for a bite at the underground snack bar before being whisked back to ground level by a wooden elevator.

Admission to the Wieliczka mines is by guided tour only. Individuals can join tour groups with commentaries in various languages including English and Polish (advance booking is recommended to avoid waiting to join a tour in the language of your choice). To get to Wieliczka, the cheapest and most efficient means is to take a contrabus marked Wieliczka–Kraków at the train station in Kraków.

Auschwitz and Birkenau

Poland was ground zero for Nazi Germany's terrible campaign to rid the world of all Jews, and Auschwitz concentration camp was one of the most efficient elements in their killing machine. Visiting it and the neighbouring Birkenau camp is a chilling and unforgettable experience. Both Auschwitz (or Auschwitz I to give it its proper name) and Birkenau (Auschwitz II) are in the town of Oświęcim (Auschwitz being

Getting there

To get to Auschwitz, you can take a 2-hour train or frequent bus (90 minutes; Nos 2–5 or 24–30) leaving from in front of Kraków's train station. However, you will need to take a taxi or walk to Birkenau from Auschwitz, as there is no frequent bus service. Alternatively, you could sign up for one of the many package tours offered by any travel agency in Kraków.

the Germanised version of the name), 75km (47 miles) west of Kraków.

At Birkenau, an inscription bluntly reads: 'Forever let this place be a cry of despair and a warning to Humanity, where the Nazis murdered about one and a half million men, women, and children, mainly Jews from various countries of Europe.' The horrors of the acts that were carried out here, and the reality of lost lives and potential, are unfathomable.

Auschwitz ❸ (daily Apr, Oct 8am–5pm; May, Sept 8am–6pm; June–Aug 8am–7pm; Mar, Nov 8am–4pm; Dec–Feb 8am–3pm; free; www.auschwitz.org.pl) was originally a Polish army barracks. Jews from as far away as Norway and Greece were loaded into wretched, sealed trains with no water, food or lavatories, and very little air to breathe, and herded to the concentration camps in Poland. The first 728 'prisoners of war,' most of them Polish and all of them from the town of Tarnów, were brought here in June 1940. After that, streams of Jews, as well as Soviet prisoners, were relocated to the camps. They became slave labourers; many died of starvation, while some were summarily executed and many others were herded into gas chambers and killed with lethal Zyklon B gas.

A short and disturbing documentary film is shown in English, German and French at regular intervals. It features original footage, shot by the Soviet troops who liberated the camp in 1945, and is a good, if startling, introduction for trying to comprehend what you're about to see. After viewing the film, pass under the famous gates of entry to Auschwitz, which are inscribed with the cruel slogan Arbeit Macht Frei (Work Makes Free).

About 30 cell blocks, as well as watchtowers and barbed-wire fences, survived the Nazi attempt to destroy the camp when they fled at the conclusion of the war. You can walk freely among the blocks and enter those that are open. In one, behind glass cases you'll see collections of piles of shoes, twisted spectacles, tons of human hair, and suitcases with the names and addresses of prisoners – who were told they were simply being relocated to a new town – stencilled on them. Hallways are lined with rows of mug shots of the prisoners, some adorned with flowers from surviving family members. Outside Block 11, the so-called 'Block of Death', is an execution wall where prisoners were shot. Inside is where the Nazis carried out their first experiments gassing prisoners with Zyklon B. Another barrack nearby is dedicated to the 'Martyrdom of

Lookout tower and barbed wire, Auschwitz

Birkenau

the Jewish People'. At the end of the exhibit of historical documents and photographs, a haunting and mournful soundtrack plays while the names of people killed at death camps are read.

Birkenau (same hours as Auschwitz I, visitors may take a bus or walk between the two; free), about 3km (2 miles) from Auschwitz, was built in 1941 when Hitler went beyond simply collecting political prisoners and embarked on a mass extermination programme. Its 300 long barracks on 175 hectares (523 acres) served as holding cells for the most murderous machinery of Hitler's extermination 'solution' for the Jews. Approximately three-quarters of all the Jews deported to Birkenau were gassed upon arrival. It was the very definition of a death camp: it had its own railway station for transporting prisoners, four huge gas chambers, each of which was capable of gassing 2,000 prisoners at a time, and crematoria were outfitted with electric lifts to take the bodies to the ovens.

Visitors can climb to the second storey of the principal watchtower at the entrance, from where it is apparent just how vast this camp was. Stretching out are seemingly unending lines of barracks, watchtowers and barbed-wire fences; the camp could hold a total of 200,000 inmates. At the rear of the camp, beyond a grisly pond where the ashes of the murdered were dumped, is an enigmatic monument to the dead of the Holocaust, with inscriptions in the 20 languages of the prisoners who were murdered at Auschwitz and Birkenau.

ZAKOPANE AND THE TATRA MOUNTAINS

Europe's second-largest chain of mountains after the Alps, the Carpathian Mountains (Karpaty) located along the southern border of Poland, are where many Poles go to relax. It is a beautiful area of forests, lakes, historic mountain towns and spa villages, with great options for hiking and skiing. The High Tatras are the highest range of the Carpathians, and the most attractive town is Zakopane, nearly on the border with Slovakia and Poland's unofficial winter capital. A 2-hour drive south of Kraków, Zakopane is easily reached by buses that leave frequently from Kraków's main PKS bus station; and though road traffic can be bad in peak seasons, the trains are considerably slower (4 hours).

Spectacular views near Zakopane

Zakopane

A small, Alpine-like village, **Zakopane** ❹ is undeniably appealing, with a terrific backdrop of snow-capped mountains and wooden chalets built in the distinctive local, so-called Zakopane Style. A remote mountain outpost until it began to gain notice in the late 1800s, Zakopane is popular for both winter and summer holidays, drawing more than two million visitors a year, who come here for outdoor sports and shopping opportunities. It is also a centre of Górale (mountain people) folk art, traditional mountain music, and a unique style of wooden highlander architecture that was elevated to high art in the mid-19th century by several notable artists and architects.

Zakopane chalets

The village's main drag is the pedestrian-only shopping street ul. Krupówki, where fashionable visitors parade up and down day and night. There are several interesting wooden buildings, horse carriages for hire, and sellers of folk art and local snacks. At the lower end of the promenade, the **Tatra Museum** (Muzeum Tatrzańskie; ul. Krupówki 10; Wed–Sat 9am–5pm, also Tue May–Sept, Sun 9am–3pm; charge) houses a collection of local folk art and exhibits on local flora and fauna.

At the end of ul. Krupówki, turn left at ul. Kościeliska. 200m (650ft) or so along on the right side is the old parish **St Mary of Częstochowa Church** (Kościół Matki Boskiej Częstochowskiej; ul. Kościeliska 4; daily 9.30am–4pm), a splendid, tiny rustic wooden chapel dating from 1847. Next to it is an old cemetery, **Stary Cmentarz**, populated with a fascinating array of carved wooden tombstones and

Snowy hike in the Tatras

gravemarkers, demonstrating the highly creative mountain artistry. The wooden homes nearby are excellent examples of the Zakopane Style, which features highly decorative carved wood.

Zakopane has earned a reputation as an artists' village, and there are several galleries and small museums of interest. One is the **Władysław Hasior Gallery** (Galeria Władysława Hasiora; ul. Jagiellońska 18b; Wed–Sat 11am–6pm, Sun 9am–3pm; charge). This branch of the Tatra Museum, close to the train station shows the works of the artist Władysław Hasior (1928–99), who was closely associated with Zakopane.

The Tatras

At the foot of the **Tatras**, Zakopane is blessed with one of the most spectacular landscapes in Poland. Even if you haven't come to ski, it's fun and worthwhile to take the cable car up to **Mt Kasprowy** for the splendid views of the mountains, hiking trails and ski slopes above the town. The ride in a modern cable car takes about 12 minutes long with a stop at an intermediate station. It takes you (and crowds of skiers in winter) up to the summit of Mt

Kasprowy Wierch, at 1,959m (6427ft). There you can stand with one foot in Poland, the other in Slovakia. Reasonably priced return cable car tickets give you a mandatory 100 minutes at the top, so if you don't have skis or don't plan to hike, you might want to bring a book. In summer, many people take the ride up and walk back down along a series of marked trails (about 2 hours). To get to the cable car station in Kuźnice (south of Zakopane), take a taxi, bus No. 7 from directly in front of the bus station, or a minibus across the street from the bus stop.

If you're interested in hiking excursions in the area, including everything from easy walks through valleys to hardcore Tatra excursions to beautiful lakes, enquire at the rustic-looking **tourism office** (ul. Kościuszki 17; Mon–Sat 8am–8pm, Sun 9am–5pm), near the bus station. The Tatras are for serious mountaineers only, and require special equipment and a guide. Less taxing nature spots suitable for day-long hiking include the valleys Dolina Białego, Dolina Strążyska, Dolina Chochołowska and Dolina Kościeliska.

Witkacy

Warsaw-born Stanisław Ignacy Witkiewicz (1885–1939), aka Witkacy, was a gifted and eccentric painter, photographer and playwright whose strange life is part of Zakopane legend. Accused of murdering his fiancée in 1914, Witkacy set off on a voyage of discovery that took him to Australia, from where he returned to fight the Germans, create some puzzling, drug-induced work, descend into bouts of depression and start a theatre company in Zakopane that still bears his name. Witkacy took his own life when the Red Army invaded Poland in 1939 and was buried first in a remote part of Ukraine before being returned to Zakopane in 1988. In one final Witkacy-style twist, the wrong body was returned and his corpse has been lost for all eternity.

The International Festival of Highland Culture is held every August in Zakopane. Essentially a week-long mountain folklore contest and packed-full schedule of concerts, music competitions and parades, it has been held since 1965, and provides an excellent introduction to the unique mountain culture of the Górale people.

MAŁOPOLSKA

Małopolska, or Little Poland, was once the name of the whole southeast corner of the country between Kraków and Ukraine,

The banks of the Vistula

but this area is now broken up into small provinces or voivodships. The small and agreeably sleepy town of **Sandomierz** ❺ (officially in the Świtokrzyskie province) is a handsome former trading port on the banks of the Vistula River. One of Poland's most ancient towns, it prospered during the Renaissance. Its old town, on a hill above the river, has a smattering of fine buildings, including the town hall on the Rynek, or market square, a 14th-century cathedral and castle, and St James's Church, founded in 1226 and one of the oldest brick churches in Poland. Of particular interest to visitors is the underground route that dips into a couple of dozen cellars beneath the townhouses around the Rynek.

Zamość

The small Renaissance town of **Zamość ❻** (Lubelski voivodship) is one of Poland's little gems. The Old Town has more than 100 buildings and monuments of artistic and historic distinction. The city was planned by the politician and nobleman Jan Zamoyski (1542–1605), who sought to build a perfect city, enclosed within fortifications, in the centre of the Lublin Upland. To carry out his plan, Zamoyski commissioned an Italian architect from Padua, Bernardo Morando, in 1580. The town's strategic location on important East–West trade routes resulted in considerable prosperity in the 17th century. Its fortifications were so strong that it was impregnable to the Tartars and Cossacks in the early 17th century, and was one of only three cities in Poland able to resist the Swedish Deluge of 1656.

Zamość's **Market Square** (Rynek), dominated by a large, pink town hall with a tall Baroque clock tower, is one of

Buildings on Market Square, Zamość

Poland's most splendid. To the right of the town hall are richly ornamented and arcaded houses painted vivid green, yellow, brick-red and blue, with Oriental detailing of 17th-century Armenian merchants. The other houses on the remaining three sides of the square are plainer and painted in more subtle pastels, but don't detract from the square's great harmony. On each side of the Rynek are eight houses (save the north side, which is dominated by the town hall).

On the north side of the Rynek is the **Regional Museum** (Muzeum Okręgowe; ul. Ormiańska 30; Tue–Sun, Oct–Apr 9am–4pm; May–Sept 9am–5pm; charge), which houses an array of items ranging from archaeological finds to armaments and religious sculptures, including an interesting clay model of the Zamość Old Town and paintings of the Zamoyski clan. More importantly, the museum is an opportunity to walk through the interior of two of the grand old burgher houses on the Rynek. Much of the houses' rich detailing – stone carving, frescoes around the top of rooms, and handsome wood-beam ceilings – have been well restored.

Just north of the Rynek is the former Jewish Quarter. In its heyday, Zamość was a multicultural city; Jews, Armenians, Germans, Greeks, Turks, Dutch and Italians all came to the city to trade. The former synagogue here has been restored and was recently opened as a modern cultural centre.

West of the Rynek is the large but rather plain **Lord's Resurrection and St Thomas the Apostle Cathedral** (Katedra pw. Zmartwychwstania Pańskiego i Św. Tomasza Apostoła; ul. Kolegiacka 2). To its immediate south, the **Religious Museum** (Muzeum Sakralne Kolegiaty Zamojskiej; ul. Kolegiacka 1a; May–Sept Mon–Fri 10am–4pm (when you can also enter the bell tower), Sat–Sun 10am–1pm; Oct–Apr Sun only 10am–1pm; charge) is a small, three-room collection of mostly Renaissance religious objects and paintings with curious translations into English.

On the eastern edge of the Old Town is the one surviving bastion of the seven that once formed the massive fortifications surrounding Zamość. The **Lvov Gate** (Brama Lwowska), next to a large and rather uninteresting market, is one of three original entrances to the city. Across from it is the large **Franciscan Church** (Kościół Franciszkanów), which retains none of its Baroque splendour, as it was destroyed when occupiers transformed it into a hospital and then military barracks. Today it is little more than a barren shell, though it still fills up for Mass.

Even though Zamość is a UNESCO World Heritage Site, its citizens don't yet seem quite accustomed to the curious attentions and cameras of foreign tourists in their midst. That makes it a good place to see a very pretty and exceedingly well-preserved little town where the citizens don't yet all speak English, and go about their business with little regard for the złoty of outsiders. On the other hand, if you're looking for something to do after taking in the main square and handful of streets that define Zamość's relaxed Old Town, you might be better off moving on to Kraków or Warsaw. If that's the case, there are regular bus and train services that take about 5–6 hours to either destination, though the connections from Lublin are faster and more frequent.

Kazimierz Dolny

Also in the Lubelski voivodship, the small, charming mercantile town **Kazimierz Dolny ❼**, perched on the banks of the Vistula, became wealthy from the grain trade in the 16th century. Kazimierz has become a popular day-trip from Warsaw, and is likely to be busy on summer weekends.

The Old Town is notable for several fine burgher's town houses with elaborate Renaissance stucco work around the Rynek, or Market Square, which is also distinguished by a central wooden well. A couple of small museums – the Goldsmith Museum and the fine Celejowska House telling the story of the town – are also worth exploring.

The ruins of the town's 14th-century castle, a short walk northeast of the Rynek, provide good views above the river, though they're better at the watchtower a little further up the hill and best at Three Crosses Hilltop, a steep climb east of the Rynek. You can reach it returning from the watchtower.

WARSAW

King Sigismund Vasa moved the royal court from the ancient city of Kraków to **Warsaw** ❽, on the banks of the River Vistula (Wisła) in the centre of the country, in 1596. Though Kraków would remain the cultural and spiritual heart of

The view from Three Crosses Hill, Kazimierz Dolny

Poland, the new political and administrative centre in Warsaw grew rapidly, adding wide boulevards and palatial residences to the small Old and New Towns.

Over the centuries, the city suffered from repeated invasions, occupations and destruction and had to be rebuilt on several occasions. World War II proved to be far more devastating and tragic than any of the previous conflicts; towards the end of the war, after the Warsaw Uprising and with the Soviet Red Army advancing inexorably, Hitler gave orders for the entire city to be systematically destroyed, and Warsaw was almost entirely levelled.

Miraculously, the Old Town was later studiously rebuilt, although not exactly as it was, according to old photographs, paintings and architectural plans.

Though Warsaw is the nation's capital, it usually proves less captivating to visitors than Kraków or Gdańsk. In part, this is because it is still a city in transition, leading the way for the new post-Communist Poland – Poland as a member of NATO and the European Union. Outside the Old Town, the city can be unattractive – the architecture a haphazard and sometimes ugly mix of Stalinist concrete tower blocks, older buildings in need of restoration, and gleaming modern towers, all constructed with little thought given to urban planning. Neighbourhoods are somewhat difficult to define. Still, it's a dynamic city of two and a half million people with an important Royal Way, stunningly rejuvenated historic centre, reminders of the Warsaw Ghetto and monuments of Jewish legacy, and an important cultural nucleus.

Fireman's Museum

A fun and free thing to do with children is to visit Warsaw's fabulous Fireman's Museum (Muzeum Historii i Techniki Pożarniczej; ul. Chłodna 3; Tue–Fri 9am–2pm). The door is always locked, so visitors must ring the bell. A free pamphlet in English is available inside the museum.

The Vistula divides Warsaw down the middle, but almost everything of interest to visitors is located on the west bank. The Royal Way, the focus of most sightseeing, stretches from the Old Town south to Łazienki Park and Wilanów, formerly a royal summer palace.

The Old Town and Market Square

Warsaw's **Old Town** (Stare Miasto) would be remarkable even if it hadn't been rebuilt from scratch after being razed during World War II. How extensive was the annihilation? Some historians estimate that 85 percent of the Old Town

The rooftops of Warsaw's Old Town

was destroyed. It is impossible not to marvel that within a period of around 30 years from the war's end, the entire Old Town was resurrected with abundant care for the architecture, aesthetics and soul of Warsaw. Competition for rebuilding projects was intense, and in fact, many other towns were neglected because of the resources directed to Warsaw. Incredibly, it looks, and more importantly feels, authentic, like a town with a medieval layout and Renaissance façades. The reconstructed town is a true testament to a people who refused to be defeated, even though the city's population had been reduced by more than two-thirds. Although some of the buildings only date from the mid-1950s, the Old Town was added in its entirety to UNESCO's list of World Heritage Sites in 1980.

The Royal Castle

It's probably best to begin a tour of Warsaw at the entrance to the Old Town, **Plac Zamkowy** Ⓐ (Castle Square). A tall column with a bronze **statue of King Sigismund** – who moved the capital to Warsaw – marks the square, against a backdrop of vibrantly coloured pastel town houses with red tile roofs. The fortifications that once enclosed the Old Town were dismantled in the 19th century, though you can still see fragments of them on one side of the square.

On the eastern side of the square is the massive **Royal Castle** Ⓑ (Zamek Królewski; pl. Zamkowy 4; Oct–Apr Tue–Sat 10am–4pm, Sun 11am–4pm; May–Sept Mon–Sat 10am–6pm, Sun 11am–6pm; charge, Sun free). Although a fortress

Royal Castle and Zygmund Column in the Old Town

was first established on this spot in the 1300s, the present structure is, like the whole of its surroundings, a recent 20th-century reconstruction. In 1944, it was little more than a smoking pile of rubble, with all its great interiors destroyed by bullets, dynamite and fire. Almost all the royal collection of great works of art and tapestries was stolen or destroyed,

Warsaw Rising

This museum (Muzeum Powstania Warszawskiego, ul. Grzybowska 79, tel: 022 539 7905; Mon, Wed, Fri 8am–6pm, Thur 8am–8pm, Sat–Sun 10am–6pm; charge) tells the story of the doomed Warsaw Uprising and hence of Poland's fate in World War II, with audiovisual displays as well as thousands of objects.

though it should be noted that many pieces, including furnishings, were removed for safekeeping when the war broke out. Reconstruction did not begin until 1971, and the Castle was reopened to the public in 1984.

As visitors to the castle pass through the stately rooms with excellent stucco detailing and lush works of art (some of which are copies of originals), they have to keep reminding themselves of the fact that what they are seeing was rebuilt in its entirety in the past 30 years. Fragments of original building materials, including decorative carvings and elements of stucco, were used in every possible case, and, if you look hard enough, you may be able to distinguish what is new from what is original.

The Royal Castle was the official residence of the kings of Poland from the 17th century onwards, and it is where Poland's landmark Constitution – the second oldest in the world, after that of the United States – was passed by the Sejm (parliament) on 3 May 1791. There are separate charges for visiting different parts of the castle. If time is limited it is probably best to visit the main parts of the interior on the ticket that gives entry to the upper-level Great and King's apartments (including the Great Assembly Room, the National Hall, the Throne Room, the Bedroom, the Old Audience Hall, the Canaletto Room, the Chapel and the Marble Room), so you will see the true highlights of the Castle.

The **King Stanisław August apartments** are among the most opulent rooms in the castle. On the upper level, the massive, mid-18th-century Ballroom – used variously as a concert hall, meeting and audience room, and the first room to be destroyed in 1939 – is perhaps the most stunning of all the rooms. Note the aptly named ceiling painting (a reconstruction), *The Dissolution of Chaos*.

The **Canaletto Room** showcases detailed paintings of Warsaw's Old Town architecture, by his pupil the Italian Bernardo Bellotto; these paintings survived the war and were instrumental in the capital's reconstruction efforts. In the **Marble Room**, another highlight, you'll see portraits of the

Nightlife in the Old Town

22 kings of Poland. The **Throne Room** glitters with a red-and-gold canopy of handmade silver-embroidered eagles. The originals were stolen by the Germans, but one eagle was recovered in the United States in 1991. It was bought by the Castle, and from it the entire canopy was reconstructed.

If you have more time, separate tickets will give you entry to the **Tin-Roofed Palace**, which was the apartment of Prince Joseph Poinatowski, where there is an exhibition of Oriental carpets; the Lanckoroński art collection, which includes paintings by Rembrandt; the coin exhibition and certain temporary exhibitions, though entry to the historic Kubicki Arcades and the displays about the castle's reconstruction are free.

St John's Cathedral

From Plac Zamkowy, head north along ul. Świętojańska. On the right is **St John's Cathedral** Ⓒ (Archikatedra Św. Jana), the oldest in Warsaw, dating from the 14th century. The cathedral was largely levelled during the war; though the Gothic brick exterior was rebuilt, too much of the interior was lost, and the Cathedral now looks wholly different from when the last king of Poland, Stanisław August Poniatowski, was crowned and buried here in 1764. The crypt holds the tombs of several famous Poles, among them the dukes of Mazovia, the Nobel Prize-winning writer Henryk Sienkiewicz, and the first president of Poland, Gabriel Narutowicz. St John's played a role during the 1944 Warsaw Uprising against the German occupiers. German tanks even entered the confines of the church. If you walk around the outside to the south wall, you'll see lodged in the stone actual fragments of the heavy equipment used by the Nazis to tear down the Old Town.

Around the Rynek

Head a little further north to the heart of the Old Town, the lively **Old Town Market Square** (Rynek Starego Miasta).

The compact square is one of Poland's finest, an unusually harmonious colourful ensemble of mostly four-storey 16th- to 18th-century (style) merchants' houses, each with wonderful individual Gothic, Baroque and Renaissance architectural features. It's simply an amazing story of reconstruction; it's hard to believe the square is a replica of what stood here before the war. In the centre of the Rynek are two water pumps and a statue of Syrena, the Warsaw mermaid of ancient legend. The square is popular with visitors, who frequent the many excellent, if relatively expensive, restaurants in the ground floors and cellars of several of the town houses. The area is particularly lively in summer, when it's covered with café tables, there are artists and buskers aplenty, and horse-drawn carriages trundle to and fro for the delight of the tourists.

On the northern side of the Rynek extends the **Historical Museum of Warsaw** (Muzeum Historyczne Miasta Warszawy; Rynek Starego Miasta 28–42; Tue and Thur 11am– 6pm, Wed and Fri 10am–3.30pm, Sat–Sun 10.30am–4.30pm; charge). A documentary film, *Warsaw Will Never Forget*, shows the extent of the wartime destruction, and efforts to rebuild the city. The rest of the museum extends across four floors and some 60 rooms of several neighbouring town houses, taking a detailed approach to the city's complicated history. There are city drawings and engravings, a sizeable exhibit on recent archaeological excavations, an interesting mock-up of an 18th-century burgher's house, armaments, documents of the resistance movement, Nazi uniforms and much more. The museum is an unending labyrinth, with most explanations in Polish only, and guards will make you follow its trajectory in a chronological order.

Beyond the Market Square, the cobblestone streets lead to attractive little corners, quiet courtyards and narrow passageways. It's a great place to wander, day or night, though you should of course exercise caution after dark. Don't miss the area behind the cathedral, where you'll find a small, pretty square (Kanonia) and a terrace with views across the Vistula. Northwest of the Rynek, on ul. Podwale, is the **Monument to the Little Insurgent** (Małego Powstańce), a bronze statue of a small boy half hidden under a giant military helmet and carrying an automatic rifle, a symbol of the young children who fought alongside adults in the 1944 Warsaw Uprising against the Nazis. North of the Market Square, ul. Nowomiejska leads to defensive walls, largely rebuilt, and the semicircular Gothic **Barbican**

The Gothic Barbican

(Barbakan), standing over a moat at what was the northern gate to the city. The area is a popular haunt of street artists and entertainers.

Beyond the Barbican is the **New Town** (Nowe Miasto), into which Warsaw expanded after outgrowing the walled Old Town in the 15th century. The two parts were not officially linked until the 18th century. Since it was created as a separate town, the New Town not only has a similar layout to the Old Town, it has its own parish church and town hall. There are several churches in the New Town, including the diminutive Baroque **Church of the Nuns of the Holy Sacrament** (Kościół Sakramentek) dedicated to St Kazimierz on the **New Town Market Square** ❿ (Rynek Nowego Miasta).

Look also for the **Maria Skłodowska-Curie Museum** (Muzeum Marii Skłodowskiej-Curie; ul. Freta 16; June–Aug Tue 8.30am–4.30pm, Wed–Fri 9.30am–5pm, Sat 10am–5.30pm, Sun 10am–5pm; Sept–May Tue 8.30am–4pm, Wed–Fri 9.30am–4pm, Sat 10am–4pm, Sun 10am–3pm; charge), just down the street from the Barbican. Maria Skłodowska (1867–1934), or Marie Curie as she's better known, was born here in Warsaw, though she lived most of her adult life in France. A scientist and physician, she was the first woman to teach at the Sorbonne in Paris. She discovered radium and polonium (named in honour of her native country) and the phenomenon of radioactivity. She was the first woman to win the Nobel Prize in 1903 (for physics) and in 1911 (for chemistry).

Syrena, the mermaid of Warsaw, in the city's Market Square

When you need a break from sightseeing, keep in mind that the New Town is also known for its restaurants and cafés.

The Royal Way

The **Royal Way** is the elegant 4-km (2.5-mile) route along which the Polish monarchy travelled south from their official residence, the Royal Castle, to the summer palace, Łazienki. The route is lined with palaces, churches, town houses, museums and monuments along or just off the main streets of ul. Krakowskie Przedmieście, ul. Nowy Świat and al. Ujazdowskie.

Ul. Krakowskie Przed-
mieście, the first stretch of
the route, is one of Warsaw's
classic streets. **St Anne's
Church** (Kościół Św. Anny;
ul. Krakowskie Przedmieście
68) was built in the 15th
century and reconstructed
in the Baroque style after it

Tram tours

Using one of the tram
routes in Warsaw (there
are around 30 of them in
total) is an excellent way to
get around. Tram stops and
routes are marked in red on
most city maps.

was plundered by Swedish troops. One of few major churches
to avoid devastation in World War II, its observation tower
has great views of the Royal Castle and Old Town. To take a
detour, walk a couple of blocks west along ul. Senatorska to pl.
Teatralny, which is dominated by the **Teatr Wielki – Opera
Narodowa** **F** (Great Theatre – National Opera; pl. Teatralny
1), Poland's greatest opera and ballet institution, built in 1833.
It was bombed during World War II, with only its façade surviving the blasts. It was rebuilt and reconfigured inside and
now has the largest stage in the world.

Back on ul. Krakowskie Przedmieście, as you head south,
you'll pass a **statue of Adam Mickiewicz**, Poland's revered
Romantic poet. Further south is the white neo-Classical
Radziwiłł Palace **G**, the residence of the president of Poland.
At the front are four stone lions and a statue of Prince Józef
Poniatowski, the 19th-century commander-in-chief of the
Polish army during Napoleon's Duchy of Warsaw. Across the
street is the **Potocki Palace**, now part of Warsaw University.
Past the grand Bristol Hotel, built at the turn of the 20th cen-
tury, is the 18th-century Baroque **Church of the Nuns of
the Visitation** (Kościół Wizytek w Warszawie), with a monu-
ment to Cardinal Stefan Wyszyński (1901–81), the Primate of
Poland from 1948.

West of the Royal Way, in the midst of Ogród Saski gardens,
is the **Tomb of the Unknown Soldier** **H** (Grób Nieznanego

Żołnierza). Housed within the surviving fragments of the 17th-century Saxon Palace, it was placed here in 1925 as the only section of the palace to survive Nazi bombing. The nearby Metropolitan office building was designed by noted British architect Sir Norman Foster.

South of Potocki Palace, **Warsaw University** (Uniwersytet Warszawski) is denoted by massive, handsome gates atop which perches the traditional Polish eagle. It is the capital's top institution of higher learning, in perpetual rivalry with Kraków's Jagiellonian University. Several of the buildings are former palaces; the oldest dates from 1634. The **Church of the Holy Cross** (Kościół Św. Krzyża; ul. Krakowskie Przedmieście 3), across the street from the university, is a mausoleum of sorts for famous Poles, among them the composer Frédéric Chopin. In fact, in accordance with his will, only his heart is here, in an urn; the rest of his remains lie in France.

Food fair on Nowy Świat Street, Warsaw

The statue at a fork in the road is one of Poland's other most famous sons, the great astronomer **Nicolaus Copernicus** (Mikołaj Kopernik). With his theory of a heliocentric universe, Copernicus, as Poles commonly say, 'stopped the sun and moved the earth.' Just beyond this, the boulevard becomes **ul. Nowy Świat**, one of Warsaw's most fashionable, and is lined with chic boutiques and cafés.

Set back from ul. Nowy Świat is Ostrogski Palace, site of the **Frédéric Chopin Museum** ➊ (Muzeum Fryderyka Chopina; ul. Okólnik 1; Tue–Sun 10am–8pm; charge; www.chopin.museum). This lovely palace is full of artefacts and memorabilia from the life of this outstanding classical composer. Nearby are several other palaces, of which the Zamoyski Palace (on ul. Foksal) is one of the most beautiful.

The **National Museum** ➍ (Muzeum Narodowe; al. Jerozolimskie 3; Tue–Thur and Sat–Sun noon–6pm, Fri noon–8pm; charge; www.mnw.art.pl) holds a huge collection of art – from Roman and Egyptian archaeology and medieval art to antique furniture and large galleries of Polish and European painting totalling some million objects. Continuing south past the controversial fake palm tree on Rondo de Gaulle and past pl. Trzech Krzyży, (Three Crosses Square, the third golden cross is in the hand of the statue of St John Nepomucen), Al. Ujazdowskie is lined with embassies housed in elegant palaces, and nearby are the Sejm (Polish Parliament) and two attractive parks, Ujazdowskie and Łazienkowski, the latter especially esteemed by Varsovians.

Jewish Warsaw

Thousands of Jews arrived in Warsaw in the second half of the 14th century, though they were expelled by royal decree not long after. They were finally allowed to settle in the city again in 1768, and by the start of World War II, approximately 350,000, or 30 percent, of Warsaw's citizens were Jews. It was at that time the largest Jewish community in pre-war Europe. The residential Jewish Quarter, around the Mirów and Muranów districts (between the Palace of Culture and Science and the Jewish Cemetery in the northwest corner of the city), was transformed into a ghetto by the Nazis. After the Warsaw Ghetto Uprising in 1943, German troops moved in and liquidated the ghetto.

Today only about 2,000 Jews live in Warsaw. The most obvious reminders of the former Jewish presence are the dilapidated buildings on **ul. Próżna**, their walls marked with bullet holes and other poignant reminders of devastation. A Jewish foundation has been entrusted with the restoration of these buildings, and work is set to begin. The **Nożyk Synagogue** (Synagoga Nożyków; ul. Twarda 6), still in use, is the only surviving Jewish house of prayer in the city. Another haunting symbol of Jewish martyrdom is the fragment of the **Ghetto Wall** (ul. Sienna 55), constructed in 1940.

Farther north, the **Jewish Cemetery** (Cmentarz Żydowski), which abuts the Powązkowski Cemetery and was founded in 1806, gives the overpowering impression of neglect: many

Memorial at the cemetery

of the 200,000 gravestones have toppled over and branches have grown over them. It seems a shame, but you quickly realise that the Jewish population of Warsaw (and indeed, Poland) was obliterated during the war, and most of the people buried here in all probability simply have no family to care for the gravesites. A monument on ul. Stawki marks the spot where 300,000 Jews were transported by train from the ghetto to the Treblinka concentration camp.

On ul. Zamenhofa, the **Monument to the Heroes of the Ghetto** (Pomnik Bohaterów Getta) is a tribute to the poorly armed but valiant Jews who rose up against their Nazi oppressors in 1943. The monument, in the spot where the month-long fighting was heaviest, is a bas-relief that incorporates stone that had been ordered by the Third Reich to commemorate its planned victory.

Monument to the Heroes of the Ghetto

West of the Old Town

The **Powązkowski Cemetery** (Cmentarz Powązkowski; ul. Powàzkowska 14) is Warsaw's oldest, largest and most spectacular necropolis, with a host of Warsaw's and Poland's most distinguished citizens, from presidents to poets, in their final resting places. The cemetery is jam-packed with gravestones and mausoleums of all shapes and sizes, many obvious testaments to the wealth and prestige of those they shelter. Some are grand, some restrained, some crowned by beautifully expressive sculpture, but all are covered by a dense, light green moss.

Warsaw's **New City Centre**, near the central train station (Warszawa Centralna), roughly equidistant between the Old Town and Łazienki Park, is a busy commercial area, teeming with banks, hotels and shops, and thick with traffic. It's

A gondola ride in Łazienki Park

perhaps most notable for the presence of a building that has become a symbol of the city, despite being abhorred by almost all Varsovians. The **Palace of Culture and Science** ⓛ (Pałac Kultury i Nauki; pl. Defilad 1), a 1955 Stalinist edifice that was ostensibly a gift of the Russian government to the Polish people, is Warsaw's tallest building, at 231m (758ft). Inside are many shops and galleries, and an observation deck on the 30th floor affords views of the entire city and surrounding Mazovian plains – when not obscured by smog. Since the collapse of Communism, there has been much debate about what to do with this unpopular building.

Łazienki Palace

The magnificent **Łazienki Palace and Garden Complex** Ⓜ (Łazienki Królewskie; ul. Agrykoli 1; Tue–Sun 9am–4pm; Palace on the Water 9am–6pm Thur–Sun; charge) is the former summer residence of King Stanisław August

Poniatowski, Poland's final monarch. At the time of its completion in 1793, the so-called Palace on the Water was far removed from the capital. Today, though, the 74-hectare (183-acre) park, opened to the public in 1818, lies right on the fringes of downtown Warsaw. The original 17th-century bathing pavilion was reshaped by the Italian architect Dominic Merlini into a magnificent Classical palace. Other buildings, including a theatre and the White House (Biały Dom) villa, along with several pavilions, orangeries, paths and canals, were added, transforming the complex into a handsome mixture of French classical and Baroque architecture and English-style gardens. The peaceful park is a favourite place to stroll for many inhabitants.

In the main building, the Palace on the Island, the neo-Classical Ballroom, Salamon Room and Art Gallery, which once displayed some 2,500 works of art (the most valuable of which were stolen or destroyed, though it still contains pieces from the collection of Stanisław August), are especially notable, as is the Dining Room, where the king held his celebrated 'Thursday dinners' with cultural and political figures. The Bacchus Room is decorated with original Delft tiles.

At the opposite end of the park, overlooking the Vistula Escarpment, is a recreation of the 1926 Secessionist **Monument to Frédéric Chopin**, depicting the composer under a willow tree, which is made to look like his piano-playing hand. The monument – which was reportedly the first destroyed by the Nazis – forms a popular outdoor venue for summer concerts.

Chopin in summer

If you are visiting Warsaw in summer, visit the Monument to Frédéric Chopin on a Sunday afternoon, when concerts are held. The combination of the statue, lake and surrounding park create an ideal setting for Chopin's romantic music.

WILANÓW

About 6km (4 miles) south of Łazienki is **Wilanów Palace** (Pałac w Wilanowie; ul. Potockiego 10–16, Wilanów; Feb–Apr and Sept–mid-Dec Mon and Wed–Sat 9.30am–4pm, Sun 10.30am–4pm; May–Sept Mon and Sat 9.30am–6pm, Wed 9.30am–8pm, Tue, Thur, Fri 9.30am–4pm, Sun 1030am–6pm charge; www.wilanow-palac.pl), another royal summer residence, dating from 1679. Originally a grand old manor house, this Baroque gem was modelled on Versailles and surrounded by magnificent gardens. Villa Nova (which became 'Wilanów' in Polish) was the favourite spot of King John III Sobieski, who saved Vienna from the Turks in 1683. After his death, Wilanów was passed among a long line of Polish aristocratic occupants, who altered and extended it. Wilanów was the last private residence nationalised by the new Communist government after

Sundial on the exterior of Wilanów Palace

World War II. The Czartoryski family, the noble family of art collectors that bequeathed their palace-museum to the city of Kraków, was one of the owners.

Even though many of the most valuable works of art were either stolen or destroyed, the palace, which didn't suffer great damage during World War II, still contains one of the largest collections of Polish portraits from the 16th to 19th centuries. The ground floor of the palace is the most opulent; the Great Crimson Room is a dining hall disguised as a painting gallery. After your tour, be sure to walk around the Italian gardens, noticing the palace's fine Baroque exterior decoration, the English-Chinese park, and the pond and Roman bridge. Near the entrance to the palace grounds, somewhat incongruously, sits the **Poster Museum** (Muzeum Plakatu; ul. Potockiego 10–16, Wilanów; Tue–Sun 10am–4pm, Mon noon–4pm; charge), dedicated to high-quality international poster art, a medium still highly respected today.

ŁÓDŹ

With approximately 750,000 inhabitants, **Łódź ❾** (pronounced 'woodge'), about 110km (70 miles) southwest of Warsaw, is the third-largest city in Poland, with light industry and about half of Polish textile production located within its boundaries. Łódź was granted a town charter as long ago as 1423, but in 1820 still only had 800 inhabitants. Things began to change in 1823 with the building of the New Town (Nowe Miasto), the first textile workers' estate. The removal of the customs barriers between Poland and Russia led to an enormous increase in the export of textiles to Russia, and in the late 19th century Łódź became one of the world's most important textile centres.

During World War II, the Germans opened two large transit camps in Łódź for Polish prisoners-of-war, as well as a camp for Russian airmen, a camp for 5,000 gypsies from Germany,

Austria and the Balkans, and also a camp for 4,000 Polish children. Approximately 260,000 Jews were murdered in nearby Chełmno and Nerem, and the people of Łódź itself were also affected; of its 600,000 inhabitants only half survived the war.

After the war new housing and industrial estates grew up around the original districts of the town. In addition to the traditional textile industry, electrical engineering and chemical industries also came to Łódź, while in more recent times the city has begun to develop its cultural personality by encouraging the arts. The first institutions of further education were founded after the war, the most famous being the State College of Cinematic Art, Drama and Television. The University of Łódź has a Department of Polish language for foreigners.

Main Sights

Łódź's star attraction is ul. Piotrkowska, its huge, 5-km (3-mile) pedestrian street cutting the city neatly in two. Lined by some of the city's finest buildings, many of which house hotels, restaurants and bars, the summer sees the street come alive with scores of lively terraces scattered all the way

Łódź Film School

In his autobiography, Roman Polański writes: 'It was through a mere whim of history that Łódź became the film capital of Poland…after the war the capital, Warsaw, lay in ruins and…the government chose the nearest suitable town when looking for a place to establish a centre of cinematography.' Two years after World War II the Kraków film course transferred to Łódź and from then on it was here that filmmakers received their training. Polański, whose films include *Rosemary's Baby* and *Chinatown*, is probably the school's most celebrated director, but other alumni include director Andrzej Wajda (*The Promised Land, The Iron Man and Danton*) and Krzysztof Kieslowski (*The Double Life of Véronique, Three Colours: Blue, White, Red*).

down. The **Textile Museum** (Muzeum Włókiennictwa; ul. Piotrkowska 282; Tue–Wed and Fri 9am–5pm, Thur 11am–7pm, Sat–Sun 11am–4pm; charge; www.muzeum-wlokiennictwa.pl) is located here in the White Factory. It portrays the development of technology in the textile industry, and houses a fine collection of 16th-century to modern textiles from all over the world.

There are two further museums of note in the city. The **Museum of Art** (Muzeum Sztuki; ul. Więckowskiego 36; Tue 10am–6pm, Wed–Sun11am–7pm; charge; www.msl.org.pl), in the palace once

Piotrkowska Street, Łódź

owned by the Poznański family, exhibits Polish and international art from the 19th century onwards. The **Łódź Museum** (Muzeum Miasta Łodzi; ul. Ogrodowa 15; Mon 10am–2pm, Tue 10am–4pm, Wed 2pm–6pm, Thur and Sat–Sun 11am–7pm; charge; www.muzeum-lodz.pl), accommodated in another of the Poznańskis' palaces, documents the town's past, showing how it looked prior to World War II's devastation. Also on display is the memorabilia of Artur Rubinstein, the famous pianist and composer, who was born here. The excellent **Philharmonic Hall** of Łódź has been named after him.

Before the war over 30 percent of the inhabitants of Łódź were Jewish. The Jewish community, both synagogues and the old Jewish cemetery were destroyed during the war. Only the new Jewish Cemetery (ul. Bracka 40, established in 1892 survived, with around 120,000 gravestones and the **Izrael Poznański Mausoleum** erected between 1903–5. Today it is allegedly the largest Jewish cemetery in Europe and one of the largest in the world.

GDAŃSK

The northern city of **Gdańsk** ❿ catapulted to the world's attention as the focus of struggles between Polish workers and the Communist regime in the early 1980s. Images of the Gdańsk shipyards were beamed into living rooms around the world. The Solidarność, or Solidarity, workers' union not only helped set in motion a movement that would eventually topple governments throughout the Soviet Union, its leader, Lech Wałęsa – a shipyard electrician – became the

Rooftops in the Old Town (Long Street), Gdańsk

first democratically elected president of post-Communist Poland in 1990.

Though Gdańsk's recent history has grabbed headlines, this city on the Baltic Sea has long been an important, and contentious, place. In 1308, the Teutonic Knights stormed the city, called Danzig by the Germans, and made it their medieval stronghold on the Baltic. It later became a prosperous port and trade centre as part of the Hanseatic League in the 14th century. For two centuries, the city essentially operated as an independent city-state. By the 16th century, Gdańsk was the largest city in Poland and the country's dominant international trade centre. During the Second Partition of Poland at the end of the 18th century, Prussia annexed the city; Napoleon laid siege to it in 1807 and declared it the Free City of Danzig; and the Congress of Vienna in 1815 returned it to Prussia.

Hitler began his acquisitive rampage here, and the assault on the Westerplatte peninsula on 1 September 1939 began World War II. The Old City, a spectacular creation of Gothic, Baroque and Renaissance architecture with a distinct Flemish aesthetic, was obliterated during the war. The city was meticulously rebuilt, and today it is one of the most spectacular of all of Poland's old cities; its Royal Way is breathtaking, even though most of it was reconstructed in the 1950s. Amazingly, Gdańsk looks and feels like a 16th-century city.

Gdańsk is in fact the largest member of a Tri-city (Trójmiasto) region on the Baltic Sea. Gdańsk, Sopot and Gdynia form a 20km (12-mile) conurbation along the bay. While the three cities have retained their own distinct identities, Gdańsk is by far the most important and historic.

The Main Town

Gdańsk is unusual among Polish cities. It has three distinct historic areas, but the Old Town is not in fact the birthplace of the city, and it doesn't possess the finest architectural ensemble. That

Golden Gate

distinction falls to the **Main Town** (Główne Miasto), often confused with the Old Town.

The Royal Way

Gdańsk, despite its tortuous history of shifting allegiances, was loyal to the Polish crown for three centuries. When the king would travel from the capital, Warsaw, to the largest port (and provider of tax income), he would enter Gdańsk through a series of formal gates and down the extraordinary main thoroughfare. Kraków and Warsaw also have Royal Ways, but neither is as stunning as the one in Gdańsk. It is one of the undisputed highlights of Poland.

The king first passed through the brick **Upland Gate** (Brama Wyżynna), dating from the 16th century, where he was given the keys to the city. Beyond the Upland Gate is the **Golden Gate** (Złota Brama), a more ornamental structure formed by an arch topped by allegorical figures. The gate was added in 1614 but only recently fully restored to its original gilded splendour. Royal processions would then proceed onto **Long Street** (ul. Długa), a pedestrian-only promenade lined with magnificent, brilliantly coloured three- and four-storey houses with fine Baroque portals, Gothic moldings, Renaissance façades, coats of arms and whimsical decorations. Most were rebuilt after World War II, which left the promenade in total ruins. A few original details did survive. Pause to admire house numbers 28, 29, 35 and 71. Of particular interest is **Uphagen's House** (Dom Uphagena; ul. Długa 12; Wed–Sat 10am–4pm, Sun 11am–4pm, Tue 10am–3pm; charge), a museum occupying a splendid 18th-century merchant's house, with displays of textiles and rich period furnishings.

At the end of ul. Długa is the 14th-century **Main Town Hall** (Ratusz Głównego Miasta; ul. Długa 46–7; Wed–Sat 10am–4pm, Sun 11am–4pm, Tue 10am–3pm; charge), crowned by a tall spire and life-size golden statue of King Sigismund August. The seat of the municipal government, it is one of the focal points of the Royal Way. The opulent interior, rich with oil paintings and frescoes, houses the **Gdańsk History Museum** (Muzeum Historyczne Miasta Gdańska; for information on the city's museums see www.mhmg.pl), where you'll find a fine collection of photographs of the city before and after World War II. The fabulous Red Room, which once held Council debates, is all original; its decorative elements were dismantled and hidden during the war. Don't miss the views of the city from the top of the tower.

Neptune Fountain, symbol of the city of Gdańsk

Just in front of the Town Hall is the **Neptune Fountain** (Fontanna Neptuna), a Flemish artist's beautiful bronze sculpture of the god of the sea, erected in 1633. It is said to be the oldest secular monument in Poland. Such was the locals' attachment to the fountain that they dismantled it piece-by-piece and hid it during World War II, finally returning it to its original place in 1954. Neptune stands at the head of the second major section of the Royal promenade, **Long Market** (Długi Targ). Several of the most attractive houses in Gdańsk face the long market, which is more a boulevard than a square. Particularly impressive is the mansion **Artus Court** (Dwór Artusa; Długi Targ 43–4; Wed–Sat 10am–4pm, Sun 11am–4pm, Tue 10am–3pm; charge), a former meeting place for Gdańsk merchants, named after the court of King Arthur. Inside the massive hall, now a museum, is an immense mid-16th-century tiled stove, with a stunning assembly of more than 500 decorative tiles.

On the same side of the street is the **Golden House** (Złota Kamienica; Długi Targ 41–2), perhaps the most beautiful in the Old Town. The four-storey structure dates from the early 17th century. The magnificent façade, thoroughly restored in 2001, is decorated with rich allegorical friezes, busts of historical figures, and at the top, four statues of gesticulating characters from classical mythology. Home to the Cunard shipping line between the wars, the building is now the Maritime Institute.

At the far end of Long Market is the **Green Gate** (Zielona Brama), a massive and bold, four-arched structure. More a building than a gate, it was intended to be a palace for visiting kings, though the exceedingly cold interior scared them away and no Polish monarch ever slept at the Green Gate.

Goldwasser

Gdańsk is famous as the birthplace of *Goldwasser* (gold water), which is vodka with added 23-carat gold leaf – once thought to have medicinal benefits. Whether the gold contributed to its flavour is a matter of opinion, but with this rich, sweet vodka, flavoured with a blend of herbs and spices, there is plenty to savour. Goldwasser was also renowned as the most expensive vodka, giving it added cachet.

Waterfront

Pass through the Green Gate and you'll discover the waterfront of the Motława River. The **Great Crane** (Żuraw, ul. Szeroka 67–68; Feb–June and Sept–Nov Tue–Fri 10am–4pm, Sat–Sun

10.30am–4.30pm; July–Aug Mon–Sun 10.30am–6.30pm; Dec–Jan Tue–Fri 10am–3pm, Sat–Sun 10.30am–3.30pm), the largest in medieval Europe, is a giant gate built in 1444 to lift massive cargo onto ships and install ship masts. The crane now forms part of the sprawling **Central Maritime Museum** (Centralne Muzeum Morskie; ul. Ołowianka 9–13; Dec Tue–Sun 10am–3pm; Jan–June and Sept–Nov Tue–Sun 10am–4pm; July–Aug Mon–Sun 10am–6pm; charge; www.cmm.pl), which expands across both sides of the river. Its buildings next to the Great Crane were exten-

Gdańsk waterfront

sively renovated, and reopened in 2012 as the Maritime Culture Centre with a collection of antique shipping vessels and boats and exhibits documenting Polish and world seafaring history, including Swedish canons from the 17th-century Deluge. A boat shuttles visitors back and forth across the Motława river when it isn't frozen, and you can also step aboard the Sołdek, the first ocean-going vessel produced by the Gdańsk shipyards and launched in 1947.

Return to the interior of the city through **St Mary's Gate** (Brama Św. Marii), a medieval defensive gate, which leads to the quiet but exceedingly evocative cobblestoned street, **ul. Mariacka**. It is one of the prettiest in Poland, with unique terraces and carved gargoyle drainpipes decorating every house.

Royal Chapel

Like others in Gdańsk, this street was reconstructed after the war, but it lost none of its charm. Many of the houses are now jewellery shops specialising in amber, the local semi-precious stone (it's actually fossilised tree resin).

The street terminates in the red-brick Gothic **St Mary's Church** (Kościół Mariacki; ul. Podkramarska 5). The massive structure, begun in the 14th century but not finished until 150 years later, is one of the world's largest churches, said to be capable of holding up to 25,000 worshippers. Indeed, it is far more impressive for its sheer size than its exterior beauty. The interior is vast but somewhat plain, a result of war damage. Impressive frescoes were whitewashed. The Gothic vault interior retains 31 chapels, three dozen large windows and one amazing **astronomical clock**. The 15th-century clock features zodiac signs, phases of the moon, time and date, and a cast of characters that peep out to celebrate the tolling of the hour. Adam and Eve ring the bell, while the 12 apostles emerge from the right side. The story of the clock has a cruel twist: it is said that its maker's eyes were put out, by order of the mayor, so that he might never again build a clock to compete with this one.

In the shadow of the St Mary's behemoth is the **Royal Chapel**, a small 17th-century Baroque Catholic church with a richly ornamented exterior. It is believed to be the work of

Tylman of Gameren, a Dutch architect. The dome-topped church was built for the city's then Catholic minority to comply with the will of the Primate of Poland. At the time, Gdańsk was a mainly Protestant city.

Just west of St Mary's (Targ Węglowy 6) is the landmark **Great Armoury**. Built in 1609 at the edge of the city's medieval walls, it is a huge Renaissance building with a spectacular façade, of marked Flemish influence. A great deal of work went into designing a building that would do little more than store armaments. Restored following damage caused during World War II, it now has another prosaic inhabitant – a shopping mall. The other side, which faces Targ Węglowy, is less ornate.

Wedged into a side street at the northern edge of the Main Town is **St Nicholas' Church** (Kościół Św. Mikołaja; ul. Świętojańska 72). Unlike much of the city, the Dominican church escaped major war damage. The light interior has a quite stunning collection of 10 black-and-gold Baroque altarpieces affixed to columns on either side of a central nave. It also features a gilded, tiered high altar and impressive Baroque organ. A children's choir sings on Sunday mornings.

Old Town

The **Old Town** (Stare Miasto) developed in tandem with the Main Town, though it was never as wealthy and after the war was not as lovingly or thoroughly rebuilt. Consequently, it has fewer sights of interest, but enough for a half-day's exploration.

Of principal interest is the **Great Mill** (Wielki Młyn; ul. Wielkie Młyny 16), a terrific structure with a sloping tiled roof. Built by the Teutonic Knights in 1350, the mill was the largest in medieval Europe, and it continued to function until the end of World War II. Today, however, it is an indoor shopping mall with all manner of clothing stores. Past the small pond behind the mill and across the street is Gdańsk's **Old Town Hall** (Ratusz Starego Miasta; ul. Korzenna 33–5; Mon–Fri

9am–5pm), a 16th-century building that was labelled the pearl of the Dutch Renaissance. Designed by Antoon van Opberghen, who also designed the Great Armoury, this is where the town council met. It now contains a café and exhibition centre, but of greatest interest is the rich interior. Walk in and take a look upstairs, where you'll find the Great Hall.

Directly across the street from the Great Mill is **St Catherine's Church** (Kościół Św. Katarzyny; ul. Profesorska 3), the former parish church and the oldest church in Gdańsk, begun in 1220. The Gothic-vaulted interior is most celebrated for the enormous mural, on the left aisle beneath the organ loft, depicting Christ's entry into Jerusalem. The church tower holds a 37-bell carillon that chimes on the hour. The church was damaged by fire in 2006, and access is currently limited to the area under the main tower. Restoration work continues.

Directly behind, or east of, St Catherine's is **St Bridget's Church** (Kościół Św. Brygidy; ul. Profesorska 17), which dates from the 15th century, but more recently became a refuge for the Solidarity movement from the Communist government. Inside are several permanent displays related to the human rights struggles of the Polish workers' union. In fact, Lech Wałęsa attended Mass here before he became the spokesman for Solidarność. The politicised nature of the church is evident on the right aisle in a series of crosses from the 1980s strikes, the gravestone of murdered priest (and Solidarność sympathizer) Jerzy Popiełuszko, and a bas-relief history of the workers' union. More recently, work is progressing on the construction of a magnificent altar made of amber and precious metals.

A 10-minute walk north takes you to the old Gdańsk shipyards, where the Solidarity union protests took root. Today the shipyard is quiet, though there's a huge **Monument of the Fallen Shipyard Workers** (Pomnik Poległych Stoczniowców; pl. Solidarności), an evocative sculpture of crosses and anchors commemorating the 44 who were killed in the 1970 street riots against the Communists. A nearby museum called **Roads to Freedom** (Drogi do Wolności; ul. Wały Piastowskie 24; Tue–Sun 10am–5pm; charge; www.ecs. gda.pl), details the history of Solidarity, and its excellent exhibition lays out the events that led to historic change in Eastern Europe. As well as the original demands of the 1980 shipyard strike, handwritten on plywood (now listed by UNESCO) it gives visitors an insight into how hard life was in Communist times.

Monument of the Fallen Shipyard Workers

Old Suburb

South of the Main Town is the third of Gdańsk's historic districts, where the city expanded in the 15th century, now called the **Old Suburb** (Stare Przedmieście). Rebuilt after World War II devastation, there are a couple of essential sights worth checking out. The neighbourhood lies across the major road ul. Podwale Przedmiejskie.

The **National Museum** (Muzeum Narodowe; ul. Toruńska 1; Oct–Apr Tue–Fri 9am–4pm, Sat–Sun 10am–5pm; May and Sept Tue–Sun 10am–5pm; June–Aug Tue–Wed and Fri–Sun 10am–5pm, Thur noon–7pm; charge; www.muzeum.narodowe.gda.pl) is one of Poland's most important repositories of medieval art, tapestries, embroidery, gold and silverware, all housed in a vaulted former Franciscan monastery and hospital.

Hel beach

Its most famous work is The Last Judgement, a triptych by the 15th-century Dutch painter Hans Memling. The Flemish and Dutch collection also contain works by Van Dyck and Breughel the Younger.

Abutting the museum is the **Church of the Holy Trinity** (Kościół Świętej Trójcy; ul. Św. Trójcy 4), Gdańsk's second-largest church. Built in the 15th century, the well-preserved Gothic structure has a spacious white interior. Of particular interest is the high altar, comprising varied panels in a triptych.

EXCURSIONS FROM GDAŃSK

Sopot ⑪, a former fishing village just 12km (7 miles) north of Gdańsk, is one of Poland's most fashionable seaside resorts. It began as a spa town in the 18th century; little damaged by World War II, Sopot has a relaxed, elegant feel, complemented by the early 20th-century Secessionist buildings. The town attracts huge crowds of northern Europeans and Poles in summer months, drawn to the cafés, restaurants and nightclubs along the main pedestrian thoroughfare, ul. Bohaterów Monte Cassino, and its sandy beaches and waters in the Gdańsk Bay (once badly polluted – be aware that the beaches may be closed at any time depending on pollution levels). Sopot also has a 10-km (6-mile) path that runs through the park along the Baltic Sea, ideal for walking, running or cycling. Also popular are the promenade along the 1920s **pier** (Molo Południowe), Poland's longest, and the open-air **Forest Opera House** (Opera Leśna), an amphitheatre in the woods.

The next town north along the bay (some 21km/13 miles from Gdańsk), **Gdynia** ⑫, is also a former fishing village, although in the 20th century it was transformed into a large and wealthy industrial port city with boutiques, bars, restaurants and museums that draw visitors from across Poland. The majority of sights, clustered around the pier, are related to the sea and seafarers. Visit the ship museums (including the Błyskawica, a World War II destroyer, and Dar Pomorza, a 1909 three-masted frigate), or the **Aquarium** (Akwarium Gdyńskie; al. Jana Pawła II 1; daily (except occasional Mondays) Apr–May and Sept 9am–7pm; June–Aug 9am–8pm; Oct–Mar 10am–5pm; charge), which includes exhibitions on oceanography, or visit the **Town Museum** (Muzeum Miasta Gdyni; ul. Zawiszy Czarnego 1; Tue–Sun 10am–5pm; charge), which explains how Gdynia developed.

Both Sopot and Gdynia are easily reached by train (leaving every 10 minutes during the day, and less frequently late at night) from the Gdańsk Główny train station. It takes about 20 minutes to Sopot, and 30 minutes to Gdynia.

To escape the crowds, head to the tranquil **Hel Peninsula**, which stretches like a slim finger 35km (20 miles) across the bay. The string of fishing villages and sandy beaches is gaining in popularity as an easy day trip from Gdańsk, Sopot or Gdynia. Trains to Hel leave from Gdynia, and take 2 hours. For tourist information, see www.jastarnia.pl.

Alternatively, go inland to the unspoilt **Kashubia** (Kaszuby) region, a hilly land of folk art, an upside-down house and an ethnically distinct people with their own language and customs.

Malbork Castle

Poland's largest, most famous castle is **Malbork** (Zamek w Malborku; ul. Starościńska 1; Tue–Sun mid-Apr–mid-Sept 9am–7pm; mid-Sept–mid-Apr 10am–3pm; charge; www. zamek.malbork.pl), about 60km (37 miles) south of Gdańsk. The 14th-century medieval fortress, built by the Order of the Teutonic Knights on the banks of the River Nogat, gives every impression of being impregnable. It is a monumental red brick complex, with turrets, drawbridges and the most solid of walls dominating the flat plains around it.

In 1280, the Teutonic Knights built a fortified monastery, and in 1308, the Grand Master came to live in Malbork, elevating the status of the settlement to headquarters of the entire Order. The interior of the castle is astounding, a labyrinth of seemingly unending rooms and chapels. Highlights include the perfectly harmonious vaulting in the refectory, the stunning

Malbork Castle

Gothic portal known as the Golden Gate, the massive Knight's Hall and the museum collection of amber. Even after the defeat and retreat of the Teutonic Knights, the castle never fell into ruin. It became a residence of the Polish monarchs.

Inclusive visits are by guided tour only, though some parts of the castle complex can be visited on one's own. Getting to Malbork is straightforward. The train journey from Gdańsk Główny train station takes 40 minutes by express train or an hour by regular train. From Malbork town, the castle is an easy 10-minute walk. This impressive landmark is well worth the time.

During summer months, Malbork Castle stages hour-long evening sound-and-light shows in the main courtyard.

TORUŃ

In the lower Vistula Valley, 182km (113 miles) south of Gdańsk, lies the handsome, historic city of **Toruń** ⓩ. Founded by the Teutonic Knights in 1233, the medieval walled town sits on the right bank of Poland's greatest river; its positioning allowed it to rise to prominence in the 14th and 15th centuries as a Hanseatic port city. It's probably best known, however, as the birthplace of Mikołaj Kopernik – or, as most people know him, Nicolaus Copernicus, the great 16th-century astronomer.

Toruń's city council outlawed wooden buildings in the 14th century, requiring all the city's important edifices to be made of brick and stone. At the time, the city won accolades as 'beautiful red Toruń'. With a unique collection of Gothic architecture, including a ruined castle, fine churches, fortifications, a leaning tower and the home of Copernicus, Toruń is distinguished as a UNESCO World Heritage Site. Today, the historic centre is a living museum of architecture, with a growing number of cafés, restaurants and shops. It is easily covered on foot, with a day's walking tour taking in all the sights, though you obviously need longer to visit museums.

Old Town

The core of the city's **Old Town** (Stare Miasto) is its **Old Town Square** (Rynek Staromiejski). In its middle stands the dignified **Town Hall** (Ratusz), a solid Gothic brick construction raised in the 14th century, with Dutch Renaissance turrets and gables (the clock tower, formerly an independent structure, was built in 1247). Suitable for a town known for a mathematician-astronomer, the Town Hall has 12 halls representing the months of the year, 52 small rooms representing the number of weeks, and 365 windows for each day of the year. The former municipal seat of government has been almost wholly taken over by the **Regional Museum** (Muzeum Okręgowe; Rynek Staromiejski 1; Oct–Apr Tue–Sun 10am–4pm; May–Sept 10am–6pm; charge; for information on the city's museums see www.muzeum.torun.pl), which displays a fine collection of Gothic art, stained glass and Polish painting

Toruń's Old Town

amid Gothic interiors with vaulted ceilings. The top of the clock tower affords a sweeping view of Toruń's red-tile roofs and the river.

In the southeast corner of the square, in front of the Town Hall, is a statue commemorating Toruń's most famous citizen, **Nicolaus Copernicus**. Across the street is a large, extravagant 19th-century building known as **Arthur's Court** (Dwór Artusa; Rynek Staromiejski 6), formerly a meeting place for town merchants and today the site of a cultural centre. Facing the square on its east side is a pretty yellow four-storey building with an ornate Baroque façade and gabled roof. Called the **House Under the Star** (Pod Gwiazdą; Rynek Staromiejski 35; Oct–Apr Tue–Sun 10am–4pm; May–Sept 10am–6pm; charge), it's a museum displaying art from the Far East. It's also worth seeing its lush interior, which features painted ceilings and the fabulous 17th-century carved wood spiral staircase that rises three floors.

On the opposite side of the Rynek is the uninspiring 18th-century **Church of the Holy Spirit** (Kościół pw. Ducha Świętego). Between it and the Town Hall is a fountain featuring a slew of frogs and a young boy playing the violin. It represents a legend of a frightening moment when Toruń was invaded by frogs and the boy charmed them back to the woods with his violin. Just off the northwest corner of the square is the imposing **St Mary's Church** (Kościół Mariacki; ul. Panny Marii), a Franciscan monastery from the 13th century. The highlight of the interior is a series of interesting and colourful frescoes on the columns supporting the nave.

Around the corner to the north is Toruń's **Planetarium** (Planetarium im. Władysława Dziewulskiego; ul. Franciszkańska

Toruń gingerbread

Toruń is known for its traditional gingerbread, and its bakers can be pretty creative with the medieval recipe. Look for gingerbread figures of Copernicus, among other fancy creations.

15–21; charge; www.planetarium.torun.pl, see website for show times). Installed in a 19th-century gasworks, whose round shape was perfect for its needs, this is the most modern planetarium in Poland. There are a variety of different shows available daily, of which five are in English. On the ground floor is an interactive exhibition, the Orbitarium.

Across the street is Toruń's respected Mikołaj Kopernik University, also a feast of Gothic brick; its **Collegium Maius** (ul. Fosa Staromiejska 3) dates from the end of the 16th century.

Toruń's other major sights are south of the Rynek. The **Copernicus Museum** (Muzeum Kopernika; ul. Kopernika 15–17; Oct–Apr Tue–Sun 10am–4pm; May–Sept 10am–6pm;

Copernicus

One of the world's most influential astronomers, Mikołaj Kopernik (Nicolaus Copernicus, 1473–1543) was born in Toruń, the son of a prosperous merchant. The house in which Copernicus was born is now a museum detailing his life and works and houses the original edition of *De Revolutionibus Orbium Coelestium*, his revolutionary, initially very controversial, theory that the sun, not the earth, was the centre of the universe.

Copernicus is said to have studied at the Jagiellonian University in Kraków. In 1497 he went to Italy to continue his studies; it was there that he witnessed a lunar eclipse, which first led him to question whether the earth was the centre of the universe. It was not until 1543, however, that his book on the subject was published, in Nuremberg. Copernicus – who only saw a copy as he lay dying of a brain haemorrhage – dedicated the book to Pope Paul III, but the Roman Catholic Church still considered his theories to be 'subversive', and the work was banned until 1757. Yet it provided a basis for subsequent theories by distinguished astronomers including Galileo. The argument over whether Copernicus was actually Polish or German is expected to continue until the universe he first described is no more.

charge), inhabits the handsome burgher's house where the astronomer was born in 1473. The museum has a first edition of his seminal work *De Revolutionibus Orbium Coelestium* along with mostly reproductions of the great scientist's instruments, and it also features a very interesting audiovisual display of Toruń in the 15th century.

Directly south of the museum, along ul. Bankowa, are remnants of the city's fortifications. Although good portions of the walls were destroyed during the 17th-century Swedish Deluge, and other sections were torn down to allow the city to expand,

Copernicus Monument

four bastions and three gates survive. Nearby are old granaries, the Monastery Gate and the **Leaning Tower** (Krzywa Wieża; Pod Krzywą Wieżą). This last item is curious indeed; it bends noticeably in towards the street. Its structural flaw is explained away by a legend that states that a Teutonic Knight, a monk sworn to chastity, was caught *in flagrante* with a townswoman and made to build a leaning tower to show the harm of deviance from upright moral standards.

On the corner of ul. Żeglarska and ul. Św. Jana is Toruń's largest church, the 13th-century **Cathedral of Saints John the Baptist and John the Evangelist** (Katedra Św. Janów; ul. Żeglarska 16). The immense brick church took a couple of hundred years to complete. Before going in, note the

Bleat the clock

Crowds gather daily at noon beneath the tower of the Town Hall to see two mechanical billy goats emerge from the parapet in the clock tower. A 16th-century tradition, the metal goats butt horns 12 times to signal the hour.

clock on the southern side; added in the 15th century, it still functions today. The spacious interior has Gothic vaulting and a series of attractive chapels and altars. Some frescoes have been uncovered; the most interesting is the monochrome painting of the devil high at the back of the right aisle. A chapel nearby holds a medieval font in which Copernicus was baptised.

East of the cathedral are the ruins of the **Teutonic Castle**, built by the Order in the 13th century. Toruń citizens destroyed it in 1454 (and hounded the Order out of town) and it has lain in ruins since. There is just one surviving tower and a covered passageway you can walk through.

New Town

In contrast to the Old Town, the buildings in the expansion east were built mostly of wood. They didn't survive, so what remain in the New Town (Nowe Miasto) are mainly brick constructions of the 15th and 16th centuries. The **New Town Square** (Rynek Nowomiejski) is less impressive than its older counterpart, but it's worth a look. The major church in this part of town is **St James's Church** (Kościół Św. Jakuba; Rynek Nowomiejski 6), which dates from 1309 and is notable for its flying buttresses – unusual for Poland. Inside are some interesting Gothic wall paintings.

Walk west to Plac Teatralny, at the edge of the Old Town, where you'll find Toruń's major theatre, the neo-Baroque **Teatr Horzycy** (Plac Teatralny 1). The park across the intersection holds a very interesting *skansen*, or outdoor **Ethnographic Museum** (Muzeum Etnograficzne w Toruniu; ul. Wały gen.

Sikorskiego 19; Oct–mid-Apr Tue–Fri 9am–4pm, Sat–Sun 10am–4pm; mid-Apr–June Tue and Thur 9am–5pm, Wed and Fri 9am–4pm, Sat–Sun 10am–6pm; July–Sept Wed and Fri 9am–4pm, Tue, Thur, Sat and Sun 10am–6pm; charge). Dating from 1959, it displays a collection of 18th- to early-20th-century houses moved here from the surrounding region. Once a year, on a Sunday in September, the *skansen* becomes a living museum with actors playing the parts of blacksmiths and other rural workers.

Bydgoszcz

Just 45km (28 miles) northwest of Toruń and easily reached by bus and train is the charming yet overlooked city of **Bydgoszcz** , sitting in Gothic, Renaissance and Art Nouveau splendour on the banks of the Brda River, which you can explore by water tram. Highlights include the extraordinary painted interior of the 15th century **SS Martin and**

Castle ruins, Toruń

Nicholas' Cathedral, the quirky Pharmacy Museum (ul. Gdańska 5) and the handful of poignant sights connected with Bydgoszcz-born Marian Rejewski (1905–80), the mathematician who first cracked Germany's Enigma code.

POZNAŃ

Halfway between Berlin and Warsaw, **Poznań** ⑯ is the principal city of Wielkopolska, a region in western Poland that is one of the country's largest and most historic. Wielkopolska means Great Poland, a title that reflects its role in the development of the Polish nation. Wielkopolska is effectively the birthplace of Poland: in the 10th century, Prince Mieszko succeeded in uniting the Polanie (literally, 'people of the fields') and neighbouring Slavic tribes, founding the Polish state in 966.

Until the royals adopted Kraków in 1038, Poznań was in essence the capital of Poland. The city began its development on the island of Ostrów Tumski and the new town centre was begun in the 13th century. In the 18th century, it fell to the Prussians under the Second Partition and became increasingly Germanic, a trait for which it is known today throughout Poland. In modern times, Poznań is best known for a tragic episode: in 1956, a workers' strike was crushed by the Communist government, leaving at least 76 people dead and nearly 1,000 injured.

Musical interlude

The Museum of Musical Instruments (Muzeum Instrumentów Muzycznych; Stary Rynek 45–7; Tue–Thur 9am–3pm and 11am–5pm mid-June–mid-Sept, Fri noon–9pm, Sat–Sun 11am–6pm; charge) is the only one of its kind in Poland. Inside you'll find early phonographs, church and Polish-army drums, a Celtic horn, 17th-century Polish violins from Groblicz, and a pianoforte once played by Chopin, as well as odd Polish folk instruments and exotic drums from around the world.

Today Poznań is one of the most dynamic and prosperous cities in Poland, with an attractive historic core, a wealth of Gothic, Renaissance and neo-Classical architecture, and a civic commitment to business development and international trade. Citizens of Poznań are sometimes chided by other Poles for being a bit too industrious and money-minded, but their work ethic is the reason the city is second only to Warsaw in terms of international investment. Poznań draws large numbers of business visitors to its many trade fairs, but the city also enchants leisure-minded visitors, who concentrate on three primary areas: the Stary Rynek, or Old Market Square, the Ostrów Tumski island and the New Town (Nowe Miasto).

Old Market Square

In Poznań you will find the **Old Market Square** (Stary Rynek), one of the largest and finest in Poland. The

Poznań's Old Market Square

fairytale **Town Hall** (Ratusz), a fanciful construction of Italian Renaissance designed by Giovanni Battista di Quadro, replaced the original, smaller Gothic 14th-century structure, which was destroyed by a devastating fire in 1536. The building, constructed in the 1550s, features a splendid three-storey Renaissance, arcaded loggia and a classical tower, added in 1783, topped by the Polish eagle. The brilliant colours of the frieze above the loggia, depicting the Jagiellonian dynasty kings, have recently been restored to their original splendour, returning the building to its status as one of the most distinctive in Poland. Although part of that status might derive from the mechanical fighting goats which clash daily over the clock. Adding to the sites of interest, just in front of the Town Hall is a copy of a 1535 pillory, with a Rococo **Proserpina Fountain** dating from the 18th century.

The Town Hall holds the **History Museum of Poznań** (Muzeum Historii Miasta Poznania; Stary Rynek 1; Tue–Thur 9am–3pm, mid-June–mid-Sept 11am–5pm, Fri noon–9pm, Sat–Sun 11am–6pm, Sun 10am–3pm; charge). The Great Hall is a spectacular vaulted room with a Renaissance ceiling, rich with stucco decoration, coats of arms, symbols of the heavens and exotic animals. The museum displays a collection of art, medieval sculpture, distinctive 'coffin portraits' (paintings of the deceased attached to their caskets) and Poznań crafts from the 10th to the mid-20th century. In the Court Chamber, there are frescoes representing the four continents then known – Europe, Asia, Africa and America. Interestingly enough, the vaulted Gothic cellars survive from the original town hall, though at the time of writing these are closed for restoration.

Adjoining the Town Hall to the south is a row of narrow and colourful fish sellers' houses, built in the 1500s. Lining the four sides of the square are elegant and colourful arcaded burghers' houses and two magnificent palaces. Many remarkable edifices had to be rebuilt in the 1950s, following World War II, to their original Gothic, Baroque and Renaissance designs. Almost all of the Rynek's houses have vaulted medieval cellars, several of which have been converted into atmospheric restaurants. Some of the best preserved include No. 37, today the Maison de la Bretagne (Dom Bretanii), but formerly the oldest pharmacy in Poznań – and Nos 40, 41, 42 and 43. A pharmacy, established at no 41 in 1564, the White Eagle, only moved at the end of the 20th century. On the façade of the **Henryk Sienkiewicz Literature Museum** (Muzeum Literackie Henryka Sienkiewicza; Stary Rynek 84; Mon–Fri 10am–5pm; charge), devoted to the Polish Nobel-prizewinning writer, you'll see a statue of the Italian architect, Battista di Quadro, who lived in this house while building the Town Hall.

Town Hall

The 18th-century **Działyński Palace**, at the corner of ul. Frańciszkańska on the west side of the square, is a lovely classical structure painted a light shade of green and decorated with sculptures and reliefs. On top is a pelican, symbolic of Poznań's rebirth after the Partition of Poland. More spectacular than the façade is the Red Room, where 'literary Thursdays' were held in the period between the World Wars. The palace at No. 91 belonged to the Miełżyński family.

Kids photographing the
Old Market Square

The middle of the square is also occupied by a large, incongruous and unattractive 1950s- and 1960s-era pavilion, which was constructed after the war on the sites of the old cloth hall and arsenal, and houses the **Galeria Miejska Arsenał** contemporary art gallery (Stary Rynek 3; Tue–Sat noon–7pm, Sun 11am–3pm; charge). The building mars the otherwise exquisite harmony of the square, and while there have been discussions in the municipal government about tearing it down or adding façades more consistent with the Renaissance appearance of the square, any such action is unlikely.

In a passageway between the pavilion and Town Hall is the **Monument of a Bamberg Woman** in folkloric dress on the way to a well, with large jugs in both hands. The statue pays tribute to 18th-century immigrants to Poznań from Bamberg, Germany. Also of note is the **June 1956 Poznań Uprising Museum** (Muzeum Powstania Poznańskiego – Czerwiec 1956; ul. Św. Marcina 80–2; under renovation; Tue–Fri and Sun 10am–6pm, Sat 10am–4pm; charge), a small but poignant museum portraying the days of unrest in the city during that year.

One of Poznań's most stately residences is the **Górka Palace**, built in the mid-16th century and occupying an entire block on the corner of Wodna and Świętosławska streets (southeast corner of the Stary Rynek). Note the Renaissance portals; in the interior is a beautiful arcaded courtyard. The palace passed from the Górkas, one of Poznań's most powerful families, to

Benedictine nuns during the Reformation; today it is the site of the **Archaeological Museum** (Muzeum Archeologiczne; ul. Wodna 27; Sept–June Tue–Thur 9am–3pm Fri–Sat 10am– 6pm, Sun noon–5pm; July–Aug Tue–Thur 10am–4pm Fri noon–7pm, Sat 11am–7pm, Sun noon–5pm; charge), displaying a collection of artefacts dating to the prehistory and foundations of Wielkopolska as well as ancient Egypt. New excavations and restoration are ongoing at the site.

During the summer, the Stary Rynek is full of lively outdoor cafés, and concerts and performances are frequently staged here. At night the square is beautifully illuminated and a wonderful place to take a stroll.

Around Old Market Square

A block south of Górka Palace is Poznań's stunning salmon-coloured **Parish Church of St Stanislaus** (Kościół Św.

Parish Church of St Stanislaus

Stanisława; ul. Gołębia 1). A Jesuit church until 1701, it is one of the most important Roman Baroque churches in Poland. Though not greatly damaged by the war, the Baroque interior, with beautiful stucco work and murals, is in the process of being meticulously restored. Like Michelangelo's Sistine Chapel, its refurbished colours are so bright that the restoration has attracted criticism. Note the curious flat cupola that is in fact an optical illusion, giving the impression of being a dome. The church organ is an excellent 19th-century example of the work of Friedrich Ladegast.

Adjoining the Parish Church, the handsome orange-pink collection of buildings, formerly the Jesuit College, now house Poznań's municipal government.

West of the Old Market Square are several places of interest. The Baroque **Franciscan Church** (Kościół św. Antoniego z Padwy; ul. Franciszkańska 2), with its twin towers, dates from the first half of the 18th century. The interior features rich stucco work and wall paintings. Across ul. Frańciszkańska is the **Museum of Applied Arts** (Muzeum Sztuk Użytkowych; ul. Góra Przemysła 1; due to re-open with new exhibitions in September 2012; Tue–Wed and Fri–Sat 10am–4pm, Sun 10am–3pm; charge), housed inside the remains of the city's former royal castle and exhibiting historical crafts such as ceramics, glass and silver. In the 13th century, a true castle stood here, but over the centuries it was continually destroyed and rebuilt. The present building, hardly a castle at all, is a reconstruction from the 18th century.

City Centre

Further west is the main building of the **National Museum** (Muzeum Narodowe; al. Marcinkowskiego 9; Tue–Thur 9am–3pm, 11am–5pm mid-June–mid-Sept, Fri noon–9pm, Sat–Sun 11am–6pm; charge), facing Plac Wolności (Freedom Square) – which ought to be called Bank Square, given the preponderance of Polish and foreign banks here. The main building of the museum is the older one, built at the beginning of the 20th century and modelled on the Berlin Arsenal. The collection of medieval art, 16th- to 18th-century European painting – featuring Spanish and Flemish Old Masters – and contemporary Polish art by artists including Malczewski, Matejko and Wyspiański, is quite impressive. The museum's new wing, opened in 2001, isn't so new at all. It was begun in 1980, which is why it has a dated feel to it. It hosts visiting exhibitions.

Also on Freedom Square, at no 19, is the **Raczyński Library**, commissioned in the early 19th century and modelled on the Musée du Louvre in Paris. It is one of Poland's oldest public libraries.

Architecture from the days of Prussian control of Poznań can be found west of Freedom Square. Look for the

Raczyński Library

Croissant crazy

Poznań is famous for its celebrations on 11 November honouring the 4th-century St Martin. On that day only Poznańians gobble up St Martin croissants, in the shape of buffalo horns, stuffed with poppy seeds.

colonnaded **Grand Theatre** (Teatr Wielki; ul. Fredry 9), with a classical portico, and the neo-Renaissance **Collegium Minus** of the university. In front of the university is a **Monument to the Victims of Poznań, June 1956**, whose two crosses mourn the protesting workers who were killed during violent demonstrations against the Communist government.

Across the street is the monolithic **Kaiserhaus**, also called 'the castle' by locals, constructed for the German Emperor Wilhelm II (he never once came to spend the night here). The massive structure now holds a cultural centre.

Directly west of here are Poznań's international fair grounds, which date from the 1920s and are the biggest and busiest in Poland. A 10-minute walk southwest, down ul. Franklina Roosevelta, past the Poznań Główny train station and just on the other side of ul. Głogowska, is **Wilsona Park**, a green space dedicated to the US President Woodrow Wilson. Within the park is the **Palm House**, a magnificent greenhouse filled with 17,000 tropical plants and many cacti.

Cathedral Island

Poznań has its origins on the tranquil little **Cathedral Island** (Ostrów Tumski), surrounded by the rivers Cybina and Warta and only a 15-minute walk east from the Old Market Square. Indeed, as the late Pope John Paul II once said, the island – today a hushed ecclesiastical district – is 'where Poland began.'

The island's crowning glory is its **Cathedral** (Katedra; Ostrów Tumski 17). At the beginning of the 9th century, the Piast Dynasty built a settlement and castle on the island. The actual foundations of the pre-Polish state are beneath the Cathedral, the oldest landmark on the island, dating back to 968. The main part of the church is Gothic, from the 14th and 15th centuries (the roof, twin towers and most of the interior were destroyed during World War II). The unusual arcaded gallery above the altar is purely decorative. On the left rear of the altar is the **Golden Chapel** (Złota Kaplica), a riot of ornate gold decoration from the first half of the 19th century, built as a mausoleum for the two rulers who were instrumental in building the Polish state, Mieszko I and his son, Bolesław the Brave. The chapel on the right aisle has fine 1616 frescoes on the arches; in the right rear, the Royal Chapel features an epitaph to the last king buried in Poznań (all of the others were subsequently buried in Kraków). The Chapel of the Holy Sacrament holds the impressive Renaissance tomb of the Górka family. Along the aisles is a series of five unique bronze

Golden Chapel

plates, original to the Cathedral, which were discovered in 1991 in St Petersburg's Hermitage Museum and returned to the cathedral. In the Cathedral crypt are the ancient foundations of the first church on this site, excavated in the 1950s, and an archaeological museum. Though the remains of the first two sovereigns of Poland are ostensibly buried here, there's no real proof of that fact.

Malta

For leisure and sport, head to **Malta** – a lake and park district east of the Old Town. Lake Maltańskie is an artificial lake constructed in the 1950s, where there are frequent regattas, a beach and water sports, in addition to a year-round manmade ski slope and a summer toboggan run. The path around the lake is popular with runners and cyclists. Concerts and theatre performances are held in summer, and there are some good restaurants and one of Poznań's best hotels on the shore of the lake.

EXCURSIONS FROM POZNAŃ

Two popular side trips from Poznań are to a castle and palace in the towns of Kórnik and Rogalin, respectively. Both can be visited by bus from Poznań, and you can go first to Kórnik and then on to Rogalin without having to go back to Poznań first. However, the visits would be much easier and less time-consuming with your own transport.

Kórnik Castle

The **Kórnik Castle** (Zamek w Kórniku; Mar–mid-Dec; charge), about 20km (12 miles) to the southeast, was built by one of Poznań's richest, most powerful families, the Górkas, in the 15th century. The castle's modified appearance both inside and out was effected under the ownership of another important family, the Działyńskis, in the 1800s, one of whom judiciously married Izabella Czartoryska, heiress to the art treasures of that family. The castle houses their collections of art and military regalia, as well as their original furnishings. Beautiful hardwood floors and carved wood portals are found throughout. The most surprising aspect of the interior is its Moorish Hall, based on the Alhambra in Granada, Spain. The grounds beyond the castle were established as an arboretum in the 19th century, with over 2,500 species of plants and trees.

Rogalin Palace

Rogalin Palace, 13km (8 miles) west of Kórnik (May–Nov Tue–Sat 9.30am–4pm, Sun 9.30am–4pm and 10am–6pm; charge). The recently renovated 18th-century Baroque palace of Kazimierz Raczyński, the secretary of the king, it is noteworthy for its gardens and small museum. The right wing of the museum holds portraits of the Raczyński family and a mock-up of the London apartment of Edward, a diplomat. Off to the left of the main house is a gallery of 'salon paintings', including Polish artists like Wyspiański, Podkowiński and Malczewski. In the attractive English-style gardens are three massive oak trees, each about 600 years old. The trees were given the names of three dukes – Lech, Czech and Rus – who founded the Polish, Czech and Russian nations.

Rogalin Palace

WHAT TO DO

From markets stalls and shopping malls to folk bands and opera, Poland offers a wealth of shopping and entertainment opportunities to suit all tastes and budgets. This chapter surveys some of the many options available to the visitor.

SHOPPING

The demise of Communism in 1989 and the move to a free-market economy have had a dramatic impact on Poland as a shopping destination. Drab state-owned stores are a thing of the past. The pound, dollar, euro and other currencies don't go as far today as they once did, but foreign visitors and their Polish counterparts can only be pleased with the opening of trade and vastly improved selection of goods on the market. In major cities like Warsaw and Kraków, Poland doesn't lag far behind Western Europe and North America for commercial opportunities and you will find branches of many of the global chains here. Even with the end of Communism and inflation, Poland remains considerably cheaper than Western European destinations.

Where to Shop

Poland's development of a market economy has produced a proliferation of stores and boutiques, including many imported from Western Europe and North America. You can now buy most Western

The price is right

Note that the price displayed is the price that is expected to be paid – it is not the done thing to haggle in Polish shops.

Shopping in the Old Town, Kraków

Baltic amber for sale in Gdańsk

goods in large and modern department stores, speciality shops and market stalls.

For folk art and other handicrafts, start at branches of Cepelia stores, a national chain of folk art and souvenir shops in large cities. (Occasionally, they go by different names, even though locals invariably call them Cepelia.) For antiques, the dominant player is the Desa chain (though there are many smaller, independent dealers as well). Poland has a rich and thriving tradition of graphic art and the best places in the country to look for Polish posters are: in Kraków, Galeria Plakatu Kraków (ul. Stolarska 8–10); and in Warsaw, Galeria Polskiego Plakatu (Rynek Starego Miasta 23); Galeria Grafiki i Plakatu (ul. Hoża 40) and the Poster Museum (Muzeum Plakatu) at Wilanów Palace.

Speciality shopping markets include the unmissable **Cloth Hall stalls**, loaded with crafts and amber jewellery, in Kraków, whose history is as long as the city's; Warsaw's swanky, boutique-lined **ul. Nowy Świat**; and **ul. Mariacka** in Gdańsk's Main Town for amber jewellery. An interesting open-air market in Warsaw is the Koło Bazaar, in Wola. In Kraków, the best flea markets are on Sunday mornings in Plac Nowy in Kazimierz and next to Hala Targowa on ul. Grzegórzeka. In Gdańsk, the covered market (Hala Targowa) is at pl. Dominikański 1.

Good sources for local shops and markets in Warsaw, Kraków and Gdańsk are the local editions of the In Your Pocket guide, which features individual store listings. See www.inyourpocket.com for more information.

Bargaining is generally only acceptable at the large **open-air markets**, though if you ask for a discount at an antiques store or art gallery, you may well be granted one.

What to Buy

Art and antiques. You'll find excellent antique furnishings and religious art throughout Poland, though the best pieces tend to wind up in the wide spectrum of shops and galleries in Warsaw and Kraków, and to a lesser extent cities like Gdańsk and Poznań. Religious icons from the Orthodox Church in Russia can be found, as a large black market in stolen icons exists throughout Central and Eastern Europe, although officials are understandably touchy about their export, even when the item in question is not originally from Poland. Strict export restrictions apply, see Visas and entry requirements, page 179.

Ceramics and pottery. Distinctive Kashubian pottery known as Ceramika Artystyczna Bolesławiec is sold the world over but is considerably cheaper in Poland.

Amber

This attractive fossilised tree resin (not a semi-precious stone) is available in many shades, from yellow to brown, and grades of clarity. The cities near the Baltic Sea, Gdańsk and Gdynia, have an abundance of amber and excellent shops, often dealing in unique pieces. Be careful not to buy amber on the street, as it is likely to be fake; look for a sign of the Amber Association of Poland ('Societas Succinorum in Polonia', www.amber.org.pl) in shop windows as a guarantee of quality and authenticity.

A wooden figurine for sale

Folk art. Rustic Poland excels at folk art and handicrafts, including hand-carved wooden (usually religious) figures; leather goods from the Tatra Mountains; embroidery and lace; hand-painted eggs (especially at Easter); and colourful naïve art and glass paintings, especially from Zakopane.

Music. CDs from Polish composers are available in record shops in major cities. The most recognisable to Western listeners are probably composers Frédéric Chopin, Krzysztof Penderecki and Henryk Górecki, who unexpectedly scored an international best seller with his Symphony No. 3 in the early 1990s. A contemporary film composer, Zbigniew Preisner, who wrote the scores for the Polish director Krzysztof Kieślowski's films, including *The Double Life of Veronique*, *Dekalogue* and the *Three Colours trilogy: Red, White and Blue*, is worth seeking out. Of special note is a recording of the best of Preisner recorded live in the Wieliczka Salt Mines outside Kraków. You can also find recordings of Polish folk music, such as traditional *górale*, or highlander, tunes from the Tatras.

Poster art. Poster design is a thriving and valued art form in Poland, and some of the finest poster artists in the world are Polish. You'll find vintage and contemporary posters for familiar Western films and the greatest hits of theatre and opera, as well as more obscure titles. Contemporary poster designers include Górowski, Stasys (Stasys Eidrigevicius) and Wiktor Sadowski.

Vodka. For an authentic bottle of Polish vodka, or wódka (pronounced 'voot-ka'), look for Wyborowa, Extra Żytnia or any flavoured vodka, such as Żubrówka (with a blade of bison grass in the bottle) and Wiśniówka (cherry-flavoured).

ENTERTAINMENT

Nightlife in Warsaw and Kraków is very cosmopolitan, with a full range of cultural offerings, including theatre, opera, ballet and classical music. In other cities, there is less variety, though both Gdańsk and Poznań have lively programmes of fine arts. Tickets for performances are much more accessibly priced than in most of Western Europe or North America.

On the pop culture front, you'll find jazz combos and films from around the world. Big-name international pop and rock bands are now routinely including Poland in their touring schedules. You'll find a range of bars, pubs, cafés and nightclubs in the cities, as well as a handful of casinos.

Performing arts. In the principal cities, Poles are stalwart supporters of the performing arts. In Warsaw, the Great Theatre – National Opera (pl. Teatralny 1, tel: 022 826 5019, www.teatrwielki.pl) is the foremost venue in Poland for opera and ballet; Kiri Te Kanawa, Kathleen Battle and José Carreras have all sung here. For classical music concerts, the National Philharmonic Hall (ul. Jasna 5, tel: 022 551 7131, www.filharmonia.pl) and the intimate Opera

In your pocket

For schedules of opera and classical music concerts, see the local editions of the English-language publication *In Your Pocket*, www.inyourpocket.com, which contain good round-ups of nightlife in Warsaw, Kraków and Gdańsk, and *Warsaw Insider*, a free monthly publication for Warsaw.

Kraków's Słowacki Theatre

Kameralna (al. Solidarności 76b, tel: 022 831 2240, www.operakameralna.pl) are among the nation's best. There are also occasional concerts at the Royal Castle on pl. Zamkowy (tel: 022 355 5170). In Kraków, the Juliusz Słowacki Theatre (pl. Św. Ducha 1, tel: 012 424 4528, www.slowacki.krakow.pl) stages opera, as well as musicals, plays and concerts. Opera Krakówska (ul. Lubicz 48; tel: 012 296 6262; www.opera.krakow.pl) concentrates on productions of classical operas; while Kraków Filharmonia (ul. Zwierzyniecka 1; tel: 012 619 8733; www.filharmonia.krakow.pl) ranges beyond symphonies and hosts other orchestras, too. Concerts are also held at St Mary's Cathedral, SS Peter and Paul Church and on Wawel Hill in Kraków, and in summer at the Chopin Monument in Warsaw's Łazienki Park. In Gdańsk, the State Baltic Opera (Al. Zwycięstwa 15, tel: 058 763 4906, www.operabaltycka.pl) is one of the best in Poland, holding opera and symphonic concerts, while chamber music concerts are held at the Baltic Philharmonic Hall (Ołowianka 1, tel: 058 320 6262, www.filharmonia.gda.pl). In Poznań, opera is performed at the Teatr Wielki (ul. Fredry 9, tel: 061 659 0200, www.opera.poznan.pl) and classical music at Filharmonia Poznańska (ul. Św. Marcin 81, tel: 061 853 6935, www.filharmoniapoznanska.pl). Poznań is also well known for its acclaimed ballet company, the Polish Dance Theatre-Poznań Ballet (ul. Kozia 4, tel: 061 852 4242, www.ptt-poznan.pl).

Drama is staged almost entirely in Polish, tending to exclude most foreign tourists. Acting and directing are of a very high standard, though, and adventurous theatregoers who don't mind not understanding the language in order to see first-rate acting and production will find plenty of excellent performances, especially in Kraków, the epicentre of the Polish theatre world. The Stary Teatr, or Old Theatre (ul. Jagiellońska 1, tel: 012 422 9080, www.stary-teatr.pl) was Poland's first playhouse, is beautifully restored with a main stage and two ancillary stages. In Warsaw, top musicals of the Andrew Lloyd Webber variety land at Roma (ul. Nowogrodzka 49, tel: 022 628 0360, www.teatrroma.pl).

Cinema. Poland has an enviable cinematic tradition and has produced great film directors who've gone on to international success, including Krzysztof Kieślowski, Andrzej Wajda and Roman Polański. Poles are dedicated moviegoers, so in the cities you'll find plenty of subtitled Western films competing with homegrown products, showing at good, Dolby sound-equipped cinemas. Film admissions are cheap by comparison with many countries. Look out for the Warsaw Film Festival in October every year.

Clubs and bars. Poland's towns and cities teem with bars, pubs and clubs, and Poles are known as heavy drinkers. The days of hard-drinking men emptying bottles of vodka in poorly lit bars are largely a thing of the past, though, and most Poles today drink more beer (*piwo*) than vodka and other spirits. You'll find Irish and English pubs and nightclubs across Poland.

Bars in atmospheric cellars, and others above ground, have proliferated in recent years in Kraków's Old Town. With so many students in town, they're usually packed. There are so many it is difficult to single out only a few, but among the most interesting are: Prozak (pl Dominikański 6); Art Club Błędne Koło (ul. Bracka 4); Stalowe Magnolie (ul. Św. Jana 15), which has

Cafe Camelot

live music and boudoir-style backrooms; Cień (next door at ul. Św. Jana 15); U Louisa (Rynek Główny 13); and, in Kazimierz, a nightlife hub where new places are opening all the time, Alchemia (ul. Estery 5) and Pub Propaganda (ul. Miodowa 20).

The distinction between cafés and bars is sometimes difficult to ascertain, but some of the many excellent cafés in Kraków include: Camelot (ul. Św. Tomasza 17), Dym (ul. Św. Tomasza 13), the historic Jama Michalika (ul. Floriańska 45) and Café Szzafé (ul. Felicjanek 10); while Singer (ul. Estery 20) is the quintessential Kazimierz café.

For jazz and blues clubs in Kraków, try Harris Piano Jazz Bar (Rynek Główny 28); U Muniaka (ul. Floriańska 3), Klub Indigo (ul. Floriańska 26) and Piec'Art (ul. Szewska 12).

Warsaw doesn't have quite as appealing a cluster of bars in one pub-crawl ready area, but the capital certainly has its share of watering holes and cafés. It has a mini collection of Irish pubs, including Jimmy Bradley's Irish Bar (ul. Sienna 39), Irish Pub (ul. Miodowa 3) and Cork Irish Pub (Al. Niepodległości 19). Other bars are Lolek (ul. Rokitnicka 20), the elegant Column Bar in the Hotel Bristol (ul. Krakowskie Przedmieście 42–44). For cocktails try Paparazzi (ul. Mazowiecka 12). Nightclubs include Opera Club (pl. Teatralny 1), Platinum (ul Fredry 6), and for jazz and blues Tygmont (ul. Mazowiecka 6-8) and Jazzownia Liberalna (ul. Jezuicka 1-3).

Gdańsk has a selection of lively pubs in its Main Town. The coolest are Café Kamienica (ul. Mariacka 37–39) and Flisak 76 (ul. Chlebnicka 9–10). For live jazz, check out the Elephant

Club (Długi Targ 41–42) or for all kinds of music and more live happenings the studenty Klub Żak (ul. Grunwaldzka 195–197).

SPORTS

The most popular sport in Poland, as in most European nations, is football (soccer), although other sports including ice hockey, volleyball, wind surfing and skiing are also popular. Being chosen as one of the host countries for Euro 2012 signalled Poland's arrival on the sporting world map. The countryside is ideal for outdoor enthusiasts, and even though most of those destinations are beyond the scope of this guide, visitors interested in horseriding, skiing, fishing and hiking have myriad options.

Golf. If you're a golf enthusiast, head for the First Warsaw Golf and Country Club (ul. Golfowa, Rajszew, Jabłonna, tel: 022 782 4555, www.warsaw golf.pl), an 18-hole course about 30km (19 miles) outside of the capital. Perhaps the best golfing is near the Baltic Sea, at the Postołowo Golf Club (Postołowo, tel: 058 683 7100, www.golf.com.pl), 26km (16 miles) south of Gdańsk.

Hiking and walking. The vast countryside of Poland is ideal for leisurely walking and more athletic hiking. One of the best areas for both, especially for serious hikers, are the High

Windsurfing on Hel Peninsula

Skiing on Mt Kasprowy Wierch in the Tatras

Tatra Mountains around Zakopane.

Horse-riding. Equestrian holidays are becoming increasingly popular in Poland; many adventure travel operators offer them – look out for stables belonging to the Polish Equestrian Federation (Polski Związek Jeździecki). If you just want to get in the saddle for a short while, contact Patataj Horse-Riding School (Szkoła Jazdy Konnej, ul. Krótka 9, Kanie, tel: 022 758 5835) near Warsaw. There are a couple of dozen stables and riding schools in the environs of the capital; ask for additional information from tourist information centres or your hotel.

Skiing. The best place for skiing is Zakopane, at the foot of the High Tatra Mountains in southeastern Poland. Skiing is excellent, inexpensive and very popular with Poles and some foreigners on ski packages, even though facilities lag behind resorts in the Alps and Pyrenees.

Swimming and water sports. In Warsaw, the Victoria, Marriott and Bristol hotels have swimming pools. Less ritzy are these pools: Aquapark Wesolandia (ul. Wspólna 4, tel: 022 773 9191, www.wesolandia.pl), Polna (ul. Polna 7a, tel: 022 825 71 34, www.osir-polna.pl) and Wodny Park (ul. Merliniego 4, tel: 022 854 0130, www.wodnypark.com.pl). Kraków also has several pools open to visitors: Park Wodny (ul. Dobrego Pasterza 126, tel: 012 616 3190, www.parkwodny.pl) is the best year-round, though open-air pools are available in summer. There are also hotel pools at the Copernicus (ul. Kanonicza 16, tel: 012 424 3400), its sister hotel the Stary (ul. Szczepańska 5, tel: 012 384 0808) and at the Novotel Kraków Centrum (ul. Kosciuszki 5, tel: 012 299 2900) and the Sheraton (ul. Powiśle 7, tel: 012 662 1000).

The most popular areas for boating and other water sports are the Mazurian Lakes district in northeastern Poland and near the towns along the Bay of Gdańsk, on the Baltic Sea.

Football. Football (soccer) is Poland's most popular spectator sport. Warsaw's two first-division football teams are Legia Warszawa (ul. Łazienkowska 3, tel: 022 628 4303, www.legia.com) and Polonia Warszawa (ul. Konwiktorska 6, tel: 022 771 7804, www.ksppolonia.pl).

CHILDREN

Travelling with children in Poland is a matter of being flexible, creative, and putting together activities to keep the kids interested when palaces, castles and rebuilt old towns impress them less than they do their parents. Many of the activities listed below are in the capital, Warsaw, where there is simply a greater abundance of facilities.

Warsaw Zoo (ul. Ratuszowa 1–3, tel: 022 619 4041, www.zoo.waw.pl) has been open since 1928. The habitats of some 4,000 animals, including Siberian tigers, kangaroos, cheetahs, crocodiles, snow leopards and an unusual red panda, are spread across 40 hectares (99 acres). The zoo also has a free-flight bird hall. Pepeland (ul. Kolejowa 378, Dziekanów Nowy, tel: 022 751 2627, www.pepeland.pl) is an entertainment park with a mini zoo and various rides about 30 minutes outside the city.

Another option for kids in Warsaw is the Teatr Guliwer (ul. Różana 16, tel: 022 845 1677, www.teatrguliwe.waw.pl).

Fountain in the Old Town, Wrocław

For children with energy to burn, there are water parks and swimming pools in summer, and ice rinks in winter. To go ice skating in Warsaw, check out the Stegny (ul. Inspektowa 1, tel: 022 842 3872, www.stegny.com.pl) or Towarzystwo Łyżwiarstwa Figurowego Walley (ul. Kombatantów 60, Julianów, tel: 0515 184 555, www.walley. pl). Another activity that is all the rage is paintball: in Warsaw, try Marcus Graf (ul. ul. Brzeska 13, tel: 0602 635 539, www.marcusgraf.pl) or Paintballs Club (ul. Lokajskiego 42, tel: 060 266 9220, www.paintballs-club.pl). In Kraków paintballers could try SafeWar Paintball (al. Kasztanowa 1, tel: 0505 165 563, www.paintball-krakow.pl).

Another fast-paced sport is go-karts. In Warsaw, race the kids over to Pole Position (ul. Pileckiego 91, tel: 0606 339 338, or ul. Powstańców Śląskich 126; tel: 0512 597 587, www.pole-position.pl). If your kids like bowling, you'll find facilities in all the major cities. In the Malta lake district of Poznań, there are many facilities ideal for children, including a man-made ski slope and an exhilarating toboggan run.

For older kids who enjoy hiking and skiing, the area around Zakopane in the Tatra Mountains is the best in Poland. Sure to be popular with kids are the 700-year-old Wieliczka Salt Mines near Kraków (see page 57), where you first descend 378 steps, then continue through long corridors and see chapels and figures (including the Seven Dwarves) entirely carved out of salt, and finally zoom up to ground level via a fast and slightly shaky bare-bones elevator.

Festivals and Events

January Opera Rara festival, Kraków

February International Sea Shanty Festival, Kraków

March/April Holy Week religious celebrations, all Poland; Misteria Paschalia organ music fesival, Kraków

Beethoven Easter Festival, Kraków

March Festival of Contemporary Music, Poznań

April OffPlusCamera independent film festival, Kraków; Festival of Science and Art, Toruń

May International Street Art Festival, Warsaw; ProBaltica Music and Art Festival, Toruń; International Book Fair, Warsaw; Film Music Festival, Kraków; Night of the Museums, all over the country

June Old Town Summer Jazz Days, Warsaw; Floriański Fair, Warsaw; Folk Art Festival, Zamość; Dragon Parade, Kraków; National Festival of Polish Song, Warsaw; Selector Electronic and Dance Music Festival, Kraków; Midsummer's Night Wianki celebrations, Kraków

24 June St John's Feast Day, especially in Warsaw, Kraków and Poznań

June/July Festival of Jewish Culture, Kraków

July Seige of Malbork re-enactment of 1410; Baltic International Sailing Rally, Gdańsk

July/August Dominican Fair, Gdańsk

August International Song Festival, Sopot; Carillon Festival, Gdańsk; International Festival of Highland Folklore, Zakopane; Artus Jazz Festival, Toruń; Transatlantyk Film and Music Festival, Poznań; Ethnoport World Music Festival, Poznań

September Dachshund Parade, Kraków; Sacrum Profanum 20th-century music festival, Kraków

October Warsaw Film Festival, Warsaw; Free Form Music and Art Festival, Warsaw

November Explorers' Festival, Łódz; 11 November Independence Day (all over the country); St Martin's Festival, Poznań

December Nativity Crib competition, Kraków (Rynek); New Year's Eve Wow open-air club night Kraków (Rynek)

EATING OUT

Polish cuisine ranges from light and elegant to rich and hearty, invariably served in generous portions. Soups are a speciality, while potatoes and dumplings are a staple, and vegetables are available in a variety of dishes. Given its shifting borders over the centuries, it's not surprising that Polish cooking also shows the influence of several national cuisines, namely of its Ukrainian, German, Lithuanian and Russian neighbours.

Many people in other countries are familiar with common Polish dishes, such as *pierogi* (stuffed dumplings), *barszcz* (beetroot soup) and *kiełbasa* (Polish sausage), as well as menu favourites such as herrings, charcuterie or sauerkraut.

The restaurant scene in Poland, like almost everything else, has changed dramatically in the years since the fall of the

Enjoying a meal in Kraków

Communist regime. Opportunities for eating out, at least as far as fine dining was concerned, used to be rare, and shortages and rationing were common. This is no longer the case. Restaurants of all styles have blossomed in all the big towns, though traditional restaurants serving classic Polish cuisine have not disappeared, thankfully. They should be the focus of any visitor's dining habits in Poland.

Book ahead wherever possible at top-tier restaurants in Kraków and Warsaw. Many restaurants remain open throughout the afternoon, and most stay open late, until 11pm or midnight.

WHERE TO EAT

Visitors will mostly eat their meals in a *restauracja* (restaurant). These range from inexpensive eateries, where office workers take their lunch, to upmarket dining rooms frequented far more by foreign visitors and a small handful of elite Poles than by ordinary citizens; restaurants have table service.

A café *(kawiarnia)* is not strictly a coffeehouse. Most also have a menu and serve everything from snacks to full meals at all hours of the day. Another traditional eatery is the cheap, cafeteria-style, self-service creature called a bar *mleczny*, literally a milk bar. Often you can get a good, home-cooked and filling plate in one of these places for very little.

WHEN TO EAT

In Poland breakfast *(śniadanie)* is generally served between the hours of 7am and 10am. Poles typically eat bread or a roll served with butter, cheese, and ham or sausage. Eggs for breakfast are not uncommon. At most upmarket hotels, a basic international breakfast buffet will generally be served. Often you will find local pastries and possibly some foods you may not think of as usual breakfast fare.

Lunch (*obiad*), generally served between 1pm and 4pm, is traditionally the main meal of the day, a fact reflected in the quantities in which it is served. Lunch typically consists of three courses: soup, main course and dessert.

Dinner (*kolacja*) is served from early evening onwards, and it can be similar to and nearly as substantial as the *obiad* or considerably lighter, with a similar selection to what would be served for breakfast.

POLISH COOKING

Certain ingredients are essential to traditional Polish cuisine: these include fish, game, potatoes, wild mushrooms and other vegetables. One of the most distinctive flavours of Polish cooking is sourness, but dishes can also be spicy hot or sweet.

Pierogi

Some traditional dishes are cooked in lard, although oil or butter is more likely to be the norm these days. If portions are too hefty for you, order soup and then an appetiser instead of a main, and try to leave room for dessert.

The undisputed frontrunner of Polish folk dishes is the ubiquitous *pierogi*, which are originally from Russia and date back to medieval times. *Pierogi* can be sweet or

Oscypek, a smoked cheese, is a Zakopane speciality

savoury. Ravioli-like dumplings are filled with one of a variety of stuffings, including fresh cabbage or sauerkraut mixed with mushrooms; cheese and potatoes; or soft fruits in summer. Small *pierogi* are sometimes served in soups. Stuffed cabbage, called *gołąbki* or little pigeons, is another traditional dish. The leaves are filled with minced meat and rice, and usually served with tomato or mushroom sauce. Poles are also very fond of potato pancakes and potato dumplings.

On menus in restaurants, main courses frequently do not include accompaniments. Potatoes, salads and other side dishes are listed under *dodatki* and served at additional cost.

Soup

Soup *(zupa)* is immensely popular with locals and always on the menu. Most Poles think a meal incomplete without soup (some visitors may find Polish soups, on the other hand, to be complete meals). *Barszcz czerwony* (red beetroot soup) is an ancient recipe; the authentic version has a distinctive taste. It can be served clear or with cream and with small ravioli-like dumplings. Beetroot soup made with vegetable stock and served with mushroom-filled *uszki* (small ravioli) is traditional for Christmas Eve. *Żurek*, or white *barszcz*, is made from rye flour then fermented, before being seasoned. It is sometimes served with sausage or a hardboiled egg. *Chłodnik* is a cold summer beetroot soup which includes thick soured cream combined with cucumbers, radishes, chives and dill. *Ogórkowa* (dill cucumber soup) is also sour, as is *kapuśniak* (sauerkraut soup). Other soups to enjoy are *grzybowa* (mushroom soup), *szczawiowa*, or sorrel soup, and *zupa koperkowa*, which features the national herb, dill.

Hearty, healthy Polish cuisine

Starters

The classic starter (*przekąski*) is herring, which can be served in olive oil, or with soured cream, or pickled with lots of chopped onions. Poland also produces a wide range of sausages and hams, which are a speciality and a national favourite of Poles. You'll also find jellied carp, pike and smoked eel as appetisers, as well as smaller portions of favourite main courses, such as *pierogi* or potato pancakes.

Main Courses

Meat (*mięso; dania mięsne*). Poland is a nation of avid carnivores, and to most Poles, a meal of substance includes meat.

Pork is by far the most popular meat dish. The classic preparation is a pork cutlet prepared with fried onions, coated in breadcrumbs and served with stewed cabbage. Roast pork is eaten both hot and cold. Hot pot roast may be served with dried prunes. Beef is less common, though *zrazy zawijane* (beef rolls filled with bacon, dark bread and mushrooms) is a standard dish. *Flaki po polsku* (tripe stew) is thin strips of beef tripe, boiled in meat and vegetable stock and served with dark bread.

Game *(dziczyzna)* and poultry *(drób)*.
Game is very popular, as you might expect from the national affinity for meat and rich tastes. Venison *(sarna)* is usually reserved for elite restaurants, as are wild boar *(dzik)* and other 'exotic' game. Look, too, for hare *(zając)* and pheasant *(bażant)*. Chicken *(kura)* is popular and is typically stuffed and roasted. Chicken soup is another great Polish favourite, as is roasted duck *(kaczka)* with apples.

Fish *(dania rybne)*.
Fish is as popular on menus as pork and other meats, with pike, eel, perch, sturgeon and others – boiled, fried or roasted – found in most good restaurants. Carp is a particular favourite (especially on Christmas Eve), often served in aspic or Polish sauce with raisins and almonds.

Vegetarian dishes *(potrawy jarskie)*.
Vegetarian restaurants are now much less of a rarity in Poland, especially in bigger cities. Although classic milk bars began basically as vegetarian places, most have now added a few meat dishes and these old-fashioned eateries may follow the Communist-era habit of 'improving' vegetables by using lard when frying. In most restaurants, vegetable accompaniments

Classic dish

The meat dish not to be missed in Poland is *bigos*, a classic hunter's stew and the supreme Polish winter meal. It consists of fresh white cabbage and sauerkraut, usually cooked with different types of meat, game and sausage (meat and cabbage in equal proportion).

Vodka, the Polish national spirit, usually drunk neat

have to be ordered separately and can be very creative. Vegetarians should steer towards potato pancakes or dumplings stuffed with fruit, *pierogi* filled with cheese and potato, and crepes. Salads include tomato salads, sliced cucumbers in sour cream, and sauerkraut.

Desserts

Poles are great eaters of pastries and sweets. Among those you're likely to find are *eklerki* (éclairs), *napoleonki* (millefeuille), *sernik* (cheese-cake), *szarlotka* (apple cake), *makowiec* (poppy-seed roll) and *mazurek* – thin flat cakes topped with nuts and fruits.

DRINKS

Poland has begun to make wine from grapes but production is still in its infancy. However, wine is becoming more and more popular, and you will find imported wines are available in cafés and restaurants. Beware the cheaper varieties in *pierogi* places – they can be terrible – but in any good restaurant you'll probably find a range of French, Italian and Spanish wines alongside those from the New World. Prices may be steeper than you might expect.

Polish beers, or *piwo*, go well with heavy, spicy foods; except at the most formal of restaurants, it is as acceptable to drink beer with a meal as it is wine. Polish beers, usually served in tall glasses, are generally light and drinkable, although they do not enjoy the same reputation as their Czech and German counterparts. In summer, cafés may serve beer flavoured with fruit or ginger syrup, while mulled beer is as popular as mulled wine in winter. Among the best-known brands are Żywiec, Okocim, EB, Warka and Tyskie. For information on brewery tours and the Brewing Museum at the Tyskie Brewery in Tychy, 20km (12 miles) south of Katowice, see www.kp.pl.

Coffee *(kawa)* is usually served black (unless you ask for milk) or with just a dash of milk. Espresso and capuccino are widely available. Tea *(herbata)*, usually served with lemon, is drunk by most Poles.

International soft drinks are readily available. Though tap water in cities is safe to drink, its taste can leave a lot to be desired, hence mineral water *(woda mineralna)* is popular with Poles.

The National Spirit

The Poles and Russians may bicker about who created it, but vodka *(wódka)* is a staple of the Polish diet. Most vodkas are distilled from rye, but a few are made from potatoes – both types have a distinct character. It is usually clear, though you'll also find coloured and flavoured versions. Wyborowa (distilled from rye) is one of the best popular brands, with a range of flavoured vodkas; look also for Luksusowa (distilled from potatoes) and Żubrówka (which is flavoured with bison grass from the Bialowieża forest), and kosher vodkas.

Vodka is heavily ritualised. If you visit someone at home, it's polite to take a bottle, though you're not expected to empty it. Poles drink vodka neat – either in one gulp or sipped – rather than in cocktails (though Tatanka, Żubrówka vodka with apple juice is popular).

MENU READER

barszcz	beetroot soup	**kurczak**	chicken
befsztyk	beef steak	**mięso**	meat
bigos	sauerkraut and meat dish	**ogórek**	cucumber
		piwo	beer
chleb	bread	**polędwica**	beef
frytki	chips/fries	**ryba**	fish
gołąbki	stuffed cabbage leaves	**ryż**	rice
		sałatka	salad
golonka	boiled pork knuckle	**ser**	cheese
		szynka	ham
grzyb	mushroom	**woda**	water
herbata	tea	**wódka**	vodka
jarzyny	vegetables	**ziemniaki**	potatoes
kawa	coffee	**zrazy**	stuffed beef rolls
kotlet	fried pork cutlet	**zupa**	soup

Stylish bar in Kraków

PLACES TO EAT

All the restaurants below accept major credit cards except where noted. The following guidelines denote an average three-course meal for one, excluding wine and service:

$$$$** over 200zł   **$$$ 100–200zł
$$** 50–100zł   **$ below 50zł

KRAKÓW

Café Ariel $$ *ul. Szeroka 18, tel: 012 421 7920.* Open daily for breakfast, lunch and dinner. In the heart of Kazimierz, the Jewish quarter, is this charming long-established Jewish (but non-kosher) restaurant. Nightly (8pm) performances by a klezmer music trio. Great fun.

Café Camelot $$ *ul. Św. Tomasza 17, tel: 012 421 0123.* Open daily for breakfast, lunch and dinner. Fashionable and funky café popular with the university crowd – a good place to sip tea, have a beer or enjoy a light meal. Excellent salads, soups, sandwiches and desserts. Medieval cellar vibe at street level.

Chimera Salad Bar $ *ul. Św. Anny 3, tel: 012 292 1212.* A series of underground vaulted rooms, open 9am–10pm, offering inexpensive self-service salads and snacks. There is also a street-level garden for summer. Extremely popular so you may have to queue, particularly at lunchtimes. Do not confuse it with its equally excellent sibling restaurant, a few doors down, which specialises in high-class Polish traditional cooking and game in season at suitably higher prices.

Chłopskie Jadło $$$ *ul. Św. Jana 3, tel: 012 429 5157.* Open daily for lunch and dinner. The name means 'Peasant Kitchen', an apt description of this excellent chain of rustic Polish restaurants. Fun, colourful, farmhouse décor and classic, robust foods, including soups, *pierogi*, fish and meat dishes, with half-litre beers, lard to spread on your bread and accompanied by folk music – as if in the Polish countryside.

Cyrano de Bergerac $$$$ *ul. Sławkowska 26, tel: 012 411 7288.* Open Mon–Sat for lunch and dinner. An elegant cellar restaurant serving French food at French prices to the city's elite plus passing celebrities. A veritable institution if, of course, you can afford it.

Da Pietro $$ *Rynek Główny 17, tel: 012 422 3279.* Open daily for lunch and dinner. Right on the Market Square, in a delightful cellar, this is a good place to get an Italian fix without breaking the bank. Large portions and a good list of pastas.

Metropolitan $$$ *ul. Sławkowska 3, tel: 012 421 9803.* Open daily for breakfast, lunch and dinner. A sleek, cosmopolitan setting, with varnished wood, leather chairs and separate dining rooms. Chic house drinks and creative international cuisine, such as sole with lime and chilli. The best choice for when you tire of Polish dumplings.

Momo $ *ul. Dietla 49, tel: 0603 926 479.* Open daily for lunch and dinner. Wholesome, vegetarian food in a small and very informal restaurant between the Old Town and Kazimierz. One of the few places in the country to serve brown rice.

North Fish $$ *Rynek Główny 25, tel: 012 431 1987.* Open daily for lunch and dinner. Quality fish and chips including spicy battered varieties and ketchup in an ice-cream cone. Added extras not found in the UK include an alcohol licence and decent salad bar.

Padre $$ *ul. Wiślna 11, tel: 012 422 0866.* Open daily for lunch and dinner. A real gem of a restaurant tucked away in an old church cellar; the menu features a beguiling mix of decent Indian and Italian food. Good music policy too.

Pod Aniołami $$$ *ul. Grodzka 35, tel: 012 421 3999.* Open daily for lunch and dinner. A cool and elegant medieval-looking cellar with stone walls, wood tables and rugs on the walls. There's also a breezy interior courtyard for outdoor dining in summer. Specialises in local cuisine, including all kinds of grilled meat dishes.

Restauracja Szara $$$ *Rynek Główny 6, tel: 012 421 6669.* Open daily for lunch and dinner. Elegant brasserie-style setting in an historic market square building, with an adventurous range of European dishes to enjoy.

U Zalipianek $ *ul. Szewska 24, tel: 012 422 29 50.* Open daily 9am–10pm. Cash only. A piece of the countryside come to Kraków, this old-fashioned place full of old ladies gossiping over tea cups features traditional flowery folk-art murals on the walls in the style of the Małopolska village of Zalipie, excellent value potato pancakes and, during the summer, a lovely terrace in the Planty.

Wierzynek $$$$ *Rynek Główny 15, tel: 012 424 9600.* Open daily for lunch and dinner. Kraków's most famous restaurant claims to have served its first banquet in 1364. It has a modern approach to traditional Polish cuisine and the menu, which includes lots of game, is served among antiques and historic treasures in grand rooms that have welcomed many presidents and stars.

ZAKOPANE

Bąkowo Zohylina $$ *ul. Pilsudskiego 6, tel: 018 206 6216.* Open daily for lunch and dinner. This excellent highlander restaurant would be 'big fun', as my Polish friend likes to say, even if the food weren't terrific (which it is). The rustic décor – a wooden lodge with fur pelts and stuffed animals – is the perfect backdrop for dishes like sour cabbage soup and heavy portions of meat. A regionally costumed band plays mountain music with great showmanship. It's so popular that another branch has opened in the same street at 28a (tel: 018 201 2045).

Gubałówka $$ *ul. Gubałówka 2, tel: 018 206 3630.* Open daily for lunch and dinner. Quality *górale* food served inside a large wooden lodge, or outdoors on the terrace in good weather, at the top of Zakopane's funicular train ride. What the place lacks in sophistication it more than compensates for with its stunning views of the mountains.

Karczma Sabala $$, *ul. Krupówki 11, tel: 018 201 5092.* Open daily for lunch and dinner. Places like this are what Poland's mountains are all about. A super wooden villa (there are hotel rooms on the upper floors), good food, a great atmosphere and decent prices. The food is local, *górale* specialities such as *patelnia bacowska*, a rich lamb stew, are a feature of the menu. The staff are friendly and speak perfect English.

ZAMOŚĆ

Bohema $$ *ul. S.Staszica 29, tel: 084 627 1443.* Open daily for lunch and dinner. One street away from the marketplace, this restaurant in an air-conditioned vaulted basement, also has a garden for summer lunches. The menu ranges over European and Polish dishes making it a good choice whether you want a snack or a more substantial meal.

Restauracja Padwa $$–$$$ *ul. Staszica 23 (Rynek), tel: 084 638 6256.* Open daily for lunch and dinner. A cellar restaurant off the Market Square, it's like a dimly lit dungeon, with massive columns and arches and a vaulted ceiling. Though it has a vaguely pre-glasnost feel to it, with its glitzy 'drink bar' at one end, you can't go wrong with Padwa's upstanding Polish fare, such as *pierogi* and soups.

WARSAW

Adler $$$ *ul. Mokotowska 69, tel: 022 628 7384.* Open daily for lunch and dinner. This cosy, popular German restaurant revels in Wiener Schnitzel, sausages and German beers. Large portions and an occasionally noisy clientele (must be all that beer).

Blue Cactus $$ *ul. Zajączkowska 11, tel: 022 851 2323.* Open daily for lunch and dinner. When Warsaw's ex-pats, many of whom are Americans, get an itch for tasty Tex-Mex (fajitas, enchiladas), they head to this colourful and cheery place.

Champions $$$ *al. Jerozolimskie 65–79, tel: 022 630 5119.* Open daily for lunch and dinner. Like Tortilla Factory (see page 152), Champions is as much a bar as a restaurant. Part of the Marriott hotel and bursting with sports memorabilia, including a full-size boxing ring in the middle of the place and big screens for sports action, the food is mostly American and includes good ribs and vast burgers.

Dyspensa $$$ *ul. Mokotowska 39, tel: 022 629 9989.* Open daily for lunch and dinner. An absolutely terrific-looking place decked out to look like a welcoming country kitchen. Very popular and atmospheric at night, when locals and a good many ex-pats pack it to enjoy international dishes including duck *à l'orange*.

Kuźnia Smaku $$$ *ul. Mozowiecka 10, tel: 022 826 3024.* Open daily for breakfast, lunch and dinner Popular place with a pre-war ambiance, concentrating on authentic Polish and Russian dishes, such as roast sturgeon with wild mushrooms.

Le Cedre $$$ *al. Solidarności 61 and 84, tel: 022 670 1166.* Open daily for lunch and dinner. Like a scene out of *Lawrence of Arabia*, this immensely popular Lebanese restaurant (there are two branches in the same street) titillates the taste buds with a menu of spicy meat dishes served with lashings of hot flat bread and of course the obligatory bubble pipe for dessert. Belly dancing entertainment is sometimes provided.

Marconi $$$$ *ul. Krakowskie Przedmieście 42–44, tel: 022 551 1000.* Open daily for lunch and dinner. As you might expect from the opulent Bristol Hotel, this is a refined, traditional restaurant serving excellent Polish and Italian cuisine. One of the city's most luxurious and sophisticated dining rooms.

Restauracja Dom Polski $$$ *ul. Francuska 11, tel: 022 616 2432.* Elegant Polish cuisine served in a traditional villa, with its own charming garden for al fresco dining.

Różana $$$ *Chocimska 7, tel: 022 848 1225.* Beautifully decorated in an antique style, this townhouse restaurant set in a romantic garden with splashing fountains, has a wonderful selection of Polish dishes.

Suparom Thai $$$ *ul. Marszałkowska 45–9, tel: 022 627 1888.* Open daily for lunch and dinner. This is certainly the best Thai restaurant in Warsaw. Great pad Thai and many other noodle-based dishes and soups are available, served in a friendly and attractive atmosphere.

Tortilla Factory $$ *ul. Wilcza 46, tel: 022 621 8622.* Open daily for lunch and dinner. Enter from ul. Poznańska to find tortillas and other classic Tex-Mex treats in an almost gastropub setting close to the city centre. Popular with a wide range of regular locals and expats, the food here is usually eaten as an afterthought once the beers start to flow – but that doesn't stop it from being one of the best places to eat in the capital.

GDAŃSK

Bar Pod Rybą $ *ul. Piwna 61-63 , tel: 058 305 1307.* Open daily for breakfast, lunch and dinner. Now in a new location, this magnificent little restaurant serves nothing but jacket potatoes to eat either in or as a takeaway. Superb value and a visual treat, portions are both delicious and enormous. It gets busy during the week, but the wait is more than worth the effort. There's a summer garden for smokers, while inside the paintings of Old Gdańsk by the owner are for sale. Highly recommended.

Green Way $$ *ul. Długa 11, tel: 058 301 8228.* Open daily for lunch and dinner. The central Gdańsk branch of Poland's most popular vegetarian restaurant chain provides large dishes of interesting and experimental food at affordable prices to a diverse clientele of students, artists and pensioners. The best vegetarian option in town.

Kuchnia Rosyjska $$ *ul. Długi Targ 11, tel: 058 301 2735.* Open daily for lunch and dinner. A cute little café on Gdańsk's most famous street. Ideal for those visitors wishing to sample traditional, tasty meals of Russian food, served in a welcoming, folkloric setting.

Restauracja Baryłka $$ *ul. Długie Pobrzeże 24, tel: 058 301 4938.* The name means 'little barrel' and your stomach might resemble that after a traditional Polish meal here of duck with apple stuffing or one of the other dishes from the regional menu. Though there are some international dishes, too, even the salads look pretty filling. The setting is suitably traditional – near the river in an ancient part of the city.

Restauracja Pod Łososiem $$$$ *ul. Szeroka 52–4, tel: 058 301 7652.* Open daily for lunch and dinner. Acclaimed as Gdańsk's finest formal restaurant, 'Under the Salmon' is a beautifully ornate establishment that used to be the distillery of Goldwasser vodka, which is infused with flecks of 23-carat gold. Posh and plush, with a sophisticated international menu, this is *the* place in Gdańsk for a special night out.

Restauracja Targ Rybny $$$$ *ul. Targ Rybny 6C, tel: 058 320 9011.* Open daily for lunch and dinner. Appropriately next to the fishmarket whose origins go back to 1343, this restaurant has gained lots of fans since it opened in 2000. Its Kashubian dishes take their cue from the Kashubian fishwives who traded in this part of town, and the menu features monthly seasonal specials.

SOPOT

Bulaj $$$ *al. Muamuszki 22, tel: 058 551 5129.* Open daily for lunch and dinner. Almost on the beach, this restaurant subscribes to the 'slow food' philosophy but its ambitions are hardly laid-back. If you want a change from fish, there are wild boar dumplings and stewed rabbit with chickpeas on the menu.

TORUŃ

Karczma Spichrz $$ *ul. Mostowa 1, tel: 056 657 1146.* Open daily for lunch and dinner. Converted from a granary in the old town and bedecked with wooden beams, this hotel restaurant serves familiar local dishes such as you might get in a traditional Polish inn, to the accompaniment of live folk music.

Petite Fleur $$ *ul. Piekary 25, tel: 056 621 5100.* Open daily for lunch and dinner. Serving sophisticated French and Polish cuisine, Toruń's most elegant restaurant is in the brick-walled cellar of a great boutique hotel in the Old Town. With heavy ceiling beams, romantic lighting and excellent service, it's the perfect place to celebrate a special occasion.

Po Naszemu $$ *ul. Dominikańska 9, tel: 056 646 1649.* Open daily for lunch and dinner. It's all change in Toruń: the town's oldest restaurant, Pod Modrym Fartuchem, now serves Indian food, so a better bet is this place which has taken over from Pod Arsenałem. With a traditional approach to fresh and locally sourced ingredients, the cooking is contemporary, yet you will find all the Polish favourites on the menu.

Zajazd Staropolski $$ *ul. Żeglarska 10–14, tel: 056 622 6060.* Open daily for lunch and dinner. This laid-back and enjoyable family-style hotel restaurant serves reasonably good Polish fare under the attractive vaulted wooden ceilings of a 14th-century Gothic townhouse.

BYDGOSZCZ

Stary Port 13 $$ *ul. Stary Port 13, tel: 052 321 6208.* Open daily for lunch and dinner. Inside a wonderfully restored red-brick granary overlooking the Brda river, Stary Port 13 is arguably the best restaurant in town. The food is predominantly Polish, the décor includes a small working water wheel and there's often excellent traditional live music.

POZNAŃ

Bażanciarnia $$$ *Stary Rynek 94, tel: 061 855 3358.* Open daily for lunch and dinner. Beautifully decorated in an antique style, with an amazing collection of Polish classics on the menu. A superb choice, if your budget will stretch to it.

Gospoda Młyńskie Koło $$$ *ul. Browarna 37, tel: 061 878 9935.* Open daily for lunch and dinner. In a handsome old water mill in woods on the outskirts of town (five minutes from the Market Square), this folksy restaurant serves Polish grilled specialities including boar and duck stuffed with apples. Great desserts and a lovely fireplace.

Gospoda Pod Koziołkami $$$ *Stary Rynek 95, tel: 061 851 7868.* Open daily for lunch and dinner. Right on the Old Market Square, this comfortable and convenient restaurant has a simple self-service area upstairs, perfect for lunch, and an elegant dining room in the brick cellar. Polish standards are served.

A–Z TRAVEL TIPS

A Summary of Practical Information

A

ACCOMMODATION

Hotels in Poland are unofficially graded from one to five stars, and those rating three to five are of comparable international standard. In smaller cities, there is a shortage of good hotels; but there is a growing number of good three-star hotels and a few two- or one-star hotels that can be recommended. Warsaw, Kraków and other larger cities have an increasing number of top-flight, five-star hotels targeting business travellers and upmarket tourists. Several familiar international hotel brand names can be found, although home-grown independent enterprises are often more characterful.

If all the higher grade hotels are full, or beyond your budget, the best option can be to stay slightly out of town in a pension or guesthouse hotel. Other options are accommodation in private homes or a self-catering apartment. There are also more than 200 registered campsites and a network of youth hostels in the major cities. Hostels can be an excellent choice for anyone wanting simple accommodation, as some are centrally situated, eg, in Kraków, and offer one or two private rooms as well as the more usual shared accommodation in larger dormitory rooms.

It is essential to book ahead during peak season (May to October). Tourism Information Offices (including those at airports) will provide lists of accommodation.

Room prices, which should be posted at the reception desk, usually include VAT and often but not always include breakfast. Outside of the most expensive hotels, prices are generally lower than those in other European countries. Confusingly, hotels may list their prices in US dollars, euros or Polish złoty, though payment is always in złoty.

Do you have a room?	**Czy są wolne pokoje?**
How much is it?	**Ile kosztuje?**

single	**pojedynczy pokój**
double	**podwójny pokój**
without bath/with bath	**bez łazienki/z łazienką**
expensive	**drogi**

AIRPORTS *(lotnisko)*

Warsaw: International flights arrive and depart from Warsaw Chopin Airport (WAW; ul. Żwirki i Wigury 1), formerly known as Okęcie Airport, southwest of the capital. There are car-hire agencies, left luggage facilities, money exchange desks, cash machines, travel agents, a restaurant and a tourist information office. It takes about 30 minutes to get from the airport to the centre of Warsaw. A taxi will cost between 40 zł and 80 zł (more at night) depending on which one you choose. Some of the taxis waiting out front may look official, but are not and will charge exorbitant prices, so be careful.

If you need to take a taxi, call for one at the information desk: Ele Sky Taxi (tel: 022 811 1111), Sawa Taxi (tel: 022 644 4444) or Super Taxi (tel: 022 578 9800). Three buses run daily from 5am–11pm from the airport (watch out for pickpockets). The 175 stops at the Centralna train station, while the 148 goes to Praga, and the 188 passes Metro Politchnika in the city centre. Bus 331 (Mon–Fri until 6pm) passes Metro Wilanowska and the N32 night bus gets you to the Centralna train station when the other buses have finished for the night. The airport shuttle-bus service runs about half a dozen times a day, between 9am and 6pm, to major hotels and the Centralna train station. Airport Information, tel: 022 650 4220; www.lotnisko-chopina.pl.

In 2011 Wizzair moved its Warsaw base to Modlin Airport (WMI; ul. Gen. Wiktora Thommee 1a, Nowy Dwór Mazowiecki; tel: 022 346 4000; www.modlinairport.pl), a former military airfield about 35km (22 miles) northwest of the city. Other low-coast carriers will probably follow suit. There is a bus service from the airport into town and a special bus service and underground station are planned.

Kraków: John Paul II International Airport (KRK; Balice, ul. Kapitana Medweckiego 1, Balice), is 18km west of town. To get to Kraków, take one of the official PT taxis (tel: 012 191 91) waiting outside the terminal. Prices range from 50–60 zł. Alternatively, buses 292, 902 and 208 take slower roundabout routes through the suburbs to the Old Town and the train station. Tickets are cheap and you can buy them from the driver. You can catch a free shuttle-bus from outside the main international terminal doors to a platform from which a train runs direct to the city's central train station. Journey time is 18 minutes, and one-way tickets cost 10zł. Airport information: tel: 012 295 5800; www.krakowairport.pl),

Gdańsk: With flights arriving from all over Europe, Gdańsk Lech Wałęsa Airport (GDN; ul Slowackiego 200, Rębiechowo) is the third most important airport in the country, and serves not only the Tri-city area but travellers from Toruń and Szczecin, too. Fast growing in popularity, it is about 10km (6 miles) and 20 minutes' drive west of the city centre. A new terminal (www.airportbus.com.pl) offers a city centre check-in opposite the Mercure Hevelius hotel (ul. Jana Heweliusza 22) with a bus link direct to the airport for 9.90zł, or 5zł extra for a hotel drop-off. From the airport itself, buses serve local train stations: 110 for Gdańsk-Wrzeszcz; 210 for Gdańsk Główny; and 510 for Gdynia Główna; with the nightbus N3 for Gdańsk Główny. The City Plus taxi rank (tel: 196 86) is outside the main terminal entrance. The journey should cost about 50zł to 70zł, but make sure you agree a price before setting off. Airport information, tel: 058 348 11 63; www.airport.gdansk.pl.

B

BUDGETING FOR YOUR TRIP

Though prices have risen in the past few years, mainly because of the złoty's relative strength against other currencies, Poland remains one of the most inexpensive European countries to visit for tourists from Western Europe and North America. Still, visitors expecting the dirt-cheap Central Europe of the recent past may be in for a bit of a surprise. Four- and five-star hotels in Warsaw and Kraków are now nearly as costly as those in Western Europe. However, many facets of daily life remain true bargains for visitors: the highly efficient public transport system, restaurants and cafés, and museums and concert performances.

Transport to Poland. For most Europeans, Warsaw or Kraków is a short, fairly inexpensive flight or train ride away. The fast-changing market for air travel with rising taxes and fuel surcharges makes it more important than ever to shop around for your ticket. A growing number of budget carriers also offer very competitive prices.

Accommodation. Room rates in top hotels are close if not equal to what you might expect to find in other European capital cities. The approximate price of a double room in high season, in central Warsaw or Kraków: 5-star hotel 500–1,000 zł (US$150–300); 3- to 4-star hotel 400–500 zł (US$125–155); 2-star hotel or pension 250–400 zł (US$77–125).

Meals and drinks. Dining out in Poland remains a bargain except at the most upmarket and famous restaurants. A three-course meal for two people, with wine and service, in a moderately priced restaurant can cost about 100 zł (US$30); at an expensive restaurant, twice that or more.

Local transport. Public transport is inexpensive whether bus, Metro (subway) or tram (2.45–4 zł). Only taxis are relatively expensive (especially if you wind up in an unofficial taxi). Opt for public transport except in rare instances (after-hours), and always call for a taxi rather than hail one on the street.

Incidentals. Museum admission: around 5–10 zł. Entertainment: theatre, musicals and classical music concerts generally start from 20 zł.

C

CAR HIRE

Hiring a car in Poland isn't a great idea unless you intend to explore the countryside in considerable depth. Car hire is expensive: daily rates in US$, including unlimited mileage, range from $100 a day for an economy-size car, including CDW insurance. At press time, petrol (gas) cost 5.50 zł per litre. Arrangements and conditions for car hire are similar to those in other countries. The minimum age requirement is 21 and you must have been in possession of a valid licence for at least one year. US and Canadian licences are accepted as are international driving licences.

Ask if CDW insurance is included in the price. There are a few local agencies, which tend to be cheaper (though they may not speak English), in addition to the major international agencies, including: Avis (Warsaw, tel: 022 650 4872; Kraków, tel: 060 120 0702; www.avis.pl), Budget (Warsaw, tel: 022 650 4062; www.budget.com.pl), Europcar (Warsaw, tel: 022 650 2564; Kraków, tel: 012 257 7900; www.europcar.com.pl), Hertz (Warsaw, tel: 022 650 ; Kraków, tel: 012 429 6262; www.herz.com.pl), and Sixt (Warsaw, tel: 0661 999 155; Kraków, tel: 012 639 3216; www.pl.sixt.com).

CLIMATE

All of Poland is very cold in winter, and warm but comfortable in summer (it can sometimes be very hot). The best weather (and time to visit) is from May to early June and September to October. Temperatures in the highlands around Zakopane are very cold in winter. The chart below shows the average daytime temperature for Warsaw, in degrees Celsius and Fahrenheit:

	J	F	M	A	M	J	J	A	S	O	N	D
°C	-1	-2	3	12	15	18	17	18	12	12	6	1
°F	30	28	37	54	59	64	63	64	54	54	43	34

CRIME AND SAFETY

Crime has risen considerably in Polish cities, especially in Warsaw. However, the country is as safe as most others in the EU and as far as visitors are concerned, the major crime is pickpocketing (usually on buses and trams) or car theft. Take the usual precautions, especially on trips to and from the airport and the railway station, and at night. Thefts have occurred on overnight trains, especially in second-class closed compartments, though the most common occurrence is when boarding. Drug-related crimes are a particular danger.

Other cities, including Kraków, are generally safer, though always be careful in areas frequented by tourists (Wawel Hill, Market Square). The Tri-city area of Gdańsk, Gdynia and Sopot has a high incidence of muggings, sometimes in broad daylight. Car thefts, car-jackings and theft from cars are commonplace. If driving, do not pull over if another driver intimates that something is wrong with your car; it is very likely a set-up for a robbery. There are also reports of thieves opening or breaking passenger-side doors and windows in slow or stopped traffic.

D

DRIVING

To take your car into Poland you need a valid driving licence and car registration papers. Cars from most European countries (including Britain, Germany and Austria) are presumed to be fully insured, so no extra documentation is needed. To be safe, carry proof of insurance.

Road conditions. Poland is not a great place to drive your own vehicle. Although the road network in Poland is improving fast, country roads leave much to be desired. Cars often have to compete with trucks and every other vehicle on the road. An ambitious construction programme involving three major motorways crossing the country (A1, A2 and A4) is underway. By the end of 2012, eight of Poland's 10 largest cities (Gdańsk, Poznań, Wrocław, Łódź, Warsaw, Kraków, Katowice and Szczecin) will have motorways connecting them to the rest of Europe. The new motorways are toll-paying, and otherwise driving can be slow-going, especially on popular routes such as that from Kraków up to the Zakopane ski slopes.

Drivers should exercise care, particularly on roads in the countryside, which are often narrow, badly lit at night, and frequently under repair, especially in the summer months. You may find that country roads are used by pedestrians and animals as well as by vehicles. Heavy alcohol consumption can often be a contributing factor in accidents, even given the stringent laws against drinking and driving.

Rules and regulations. Drive on the right and pass on the left. Cars must be fitted with a nationality plate or sticker and use headlights at all times, night and day. A set of spare bulbs, a fire extinguisher, a first-aid kit, and a warning triangle are also obligatory. Seat belts are compulsory in all seats; children under 12 are prohibited from travelling in the front seat and must be in a car safety seat. Motorcycle riders and passengers must wear crash helmets. Using a mobile phone while driving is prohibited. Drinking and driving laws are tough; a blood alcohol level of more than 0.5 mg per litre is punishable by two years in prison.

Speed limits are 140km/h (87 mph) on motorways, 120km/h (75mph) on dual carriageways, 100km/h (62mph) on single carriageways, 90km/h (56mph) outside urban areas, and 50km/h (31mph) in built-up areas during the daytime and 60km/h (37mph) at night. You may be fined on the spot for speeding.

Fuel costs (benzyna). Petrol (gas) stations are common along highways and main roads, but don't venture down minor roads without filling up. Stations are usually open 24 hours. Unleaded fuel is widely available (about 5.50zł) and diesel and LPG are also widely available. Only in the rarest of cases are credit cards not accepted for payment.

Parking. Parking is a problem in any of the big cities, especially where historic centres are pedestrian-only. If you are driving, check that your hotel has parking facilities. A car parked in a prohibited zone will be towed away. Only guarded car parks should be used.

If you need help. If driving your own car, you should take out breakdown insurance cover; car rental companies usually have their own service. For roadside assistance, call the National Roadside Assistance Service, tel: 022 9637. Help will normally arrive within the hour. Three-quarters of breakdowns can be dealt with at the roadside, if you need a tow the charge depends on the type of repair and the towing distance. Remember to put out the red warning triangle 50m (55yd) behind your car or 100m (110yd) behind if you are on a dual carriageway. If anyone is injured, the police must be notified.

Road signs. Standard international pictographs are in use all over Poland. A sign with 'Czarny Punkt', showing a cross in a black circle, indicates a very dangerous area.

E

ELECTRICITY

The current is 220 volts AC, 50 Hertz throughout Poland. Plugs are the standard Continental, round two-pin type, for which British and North American appliances need an adapter. Electrical equipment of 110V/60Hz requires a transformer, though note than most mobile telephone and digital camera chargers incorporate a transformer.

EMBASSIES AND CONSULATES

Embassies are located in Warsaw; a few nations have consulates in other cities, notably Kraków and Gdańsk.

Australia: Embassy, ul. Nowogrodzka 11, tel: 022 521 3444 (www.australia.pl).

Canada: Embassy, ul. Matejki 1–5, 10th floor, tel: 022 584 3100 (www.canada.pl).

Ireland: Consulate (Warsaw), ul. Mysia 5, tel: 022 849 6633 (www.irlandia.pl).

New Zealand: Embassy, Al. Ujazdowskie 51, tel: 022 521 0500 (www.nzembassy.pl).

South Africa: Consulate (Warsaw), ul. Koszykowa 54, tel: 022 625 6228 (www.dfa.gov.za).

UK: Embassy, ul. Kawalerii 12, tel: 022 311 0000. Consulate (Kraków), ul. Św. Anny 9, tel: 012 421 7030 (www.ukinpoland.fco.gov.uk).

USA: Embassy, Al. Ujazdowskie 29–31, tel: 022 504 2000. Consulate (Kraków), ul. Stolarska 9, tel: 012 424 5100 (www.poland.usembassy.gov).

EMERGENCIES

The three main emergency services telephone numbers are listed below, although the chances of an English speaker at the other end are slim.
Ambulance tel: 999
Fire tel: 998
Police tel: 997
Universal emergency number from a mobile (cell) phone: 112
Between 1 June and 30 September, a special tourist helpline is in operation daily 10am–10pm; tel: 0800 200 300 (from landlines) or 0608 599 999 (from mobile phones).

ambulance	**karetka pogotowia**
doctor	**lekarz**
hospital	**szpital**
police	**policja**
Can you help me?	**Czy może mi pan[i] pomóc?**

G

GAY AND LESBIAN TRAVELLERS

As a fervently Catholic and conservative country, gay life is not much out in the open in Poland, though an indicator of changing values is that in 2011 Kraków elected Europe's first transgendered member of parliament. There are gay scenes in Warsaw and Kraków and to a lesser extent in smaller cities. Find information on gay events in Kraków on www.queerowymaj.pl. A good organisation to contact in Warsaw is Lambda (ul. Żurawia 24A, tel: 022 628 5222, www.lambdawarszawa.org). For information on gay Poland, check out www.gejowo.pl (you will need an internet translation service).

GETTING THERE

Air travel. Many European airlines serve Poland, as do several American and Canadian carriers. In all, Warsaw has flights to and from about 50 cities in 30 countries. The Polish national carrier, LOT Polish Airlines, flies from most major European cities and from North America. Scheduled flights are also available from British Airways. From the northeast coast of the US, flying time to Warsaw is about 8 hours.

International airport. Warsaw's Chopin airport is the primary international airport, though there are also international flights to Kraków, Gdańsk, Katowice, Łódź, Szczecin, Poznań, Wrocław and Rzeszow with budget airlines increasing their reach all the time.

Rail travel. Warsaw and Kraków, among other cities, can easily be reached from any major Western, Central or Eastern European city. From the UK, take the Eurostar to Brussels, change for Cologne from which you can take the sleeper to Warsaw, or change in Paris for the sleeper to Berlin, where you can catch an express to Warsaw, Kraków, Poznań, Wrocław or Katowice. InterRail and Eurail passes are valid in Poland. Both RailEurope (www.raileurope.co.uk; tel: 0844 848 40 70) and Deutsche Bahn (www.bahn.com; tel: 08718 80 80 66) book train journeys across Europe. Warsaw's international railway station is Warszawa Centralna; Kraków's is Dworzec Główny. For train information tel: 042 19 436 (within Poland) or 042 205 55 05 (from outside the country).

By car/coach. Budget airlines may be cheap for those booking ahead, but travelling by coach is still an option, especially if you want to visit several cities – either across Europe or within Poland. Eurolines (www.eurolines.co.uk; tel: 08717 81 81 77 in the UK) has daily departures from London Victoria, changing in Berlin, to all the major cities in Poland and many smaller ones. The trip costs from £79 one way. The Eurolines Pass is also available, for 15 or 30 days from £159. Buses from across Europe arrive at Warszawa Zachodnia (Warsaw West) station (tel: 0703 40 33 30). If you plan to drive across the Continent, the most direct route is via Ostend, Brussels and Berlin.

GUIDES AND TOURS

Travel agencies and organisations in many countries operate organised sightseeing tours of Poland. Look out for specialised trips, such as Jewish pilgrimage tours. Other speciality tours, which you can book on arrival, include Schindler's List tours in Kazimierz, the historic Jewish quarter of Kraków.

H

HEALTH AND MEDICAL CARE

Polish doctors and other health officials are generally knowledgeable and skilled, and most speak some English and German. Doctors and hospitals may expect immediate cash payment for health services although medical treatment will normally be provided free of charge to EU citizens who have a European Health Insurance Card (available from post offices in the UK and online at www.ehic.org.uk). Visitors from non-EU countries should obtain medical insurance, and even EU citizens may wish to insure themselves privately, for example to ensure prompt repatriation in a medical emergency.

Bottled water is inexpensive to buy, although water is safe to drink except perhaps in the deepest countryside. Many Poles drink bottled water because they prefer the taste. If you plan to spend a lot of time in country areas, particularly those close to Russia, Lithuania or Belarus, it is wise to see your doctor about the symptoms and treatment of Lyme disease.

Emergency medical treatment on the scene is available for foreigners. Ask at your hotel or consulate for the name of a doctor who speaks your language. In Warsaw, Kraków, Gdańsk, Katowice, Szczecin, Łódź and Poznań, you can call the private medical service, Falck, using the local city code followed by 19675, which can usually arrange English-language emergency services. Warsaw's Central Emergency Medical Centre is located at ul. Hoża 56 (corner of ul.

Poznańska). A private hospital with a good reputation is the Hospital of the Ministry of Internal Affairs (ul. Wołoska 137, tel: 022 508 2000). Centrum Medicover has medical centres in various Polish cities, such as Kraków, Warsaw, Poznań and Gdańsk; in emergencies tel: 1 9677 (24 hours).

Pharmacies. Look for the sign 'apteka'. In Poland these shops only sell pharmaceutical and related products. Tourism Information Offices have lists of night pharmacies. In Warsaw, two are: Apteka Przy Willowej (ul. Puławska 39, tel: 022 849 3757) and Apteka Grabowskiego (al. Jerozolimskie 54, Centralny Station, tel: 022 825 6986). Local editions of In Your Pocket (www.inyourpocket.com), list additional pharmacies.

Where's the nearest pharmacy?	**Gdzie jest najbliższa apteka?**
I need a doctor.	**Ja potrzebuję doktora.**
I need a dentist.	**Ja potrzebuję dentystę.**

L

LANGUAGE

Polish, a Slavic language, is the mother tongue of 99 percent of the population. The most widely known foreign language is German, though English is quickly gaining on it and is far more popular than German amongst the younger population. In the main cities English speakers are unlikely to encounter many problems. In the countryside, it will be more difficult. The Polish language is grammatically complicated, but it is written completely phonetically. Learning even a handful of key phrases is a good idea and will prove very helpful. As a general rule, the accent falls on the second-last syllable.

The following are a few useful phrases:

yes	**tak**
no	**nie**
Hi. (informal, singular/plural)	**Cześć (chesh).**
Good night.	**Dobranoc.**
Goodbye.	**Do widzenia.**
Thank you (very much).	**Dziękuję (bardzo).**
Excuse me (sorry).	**Przepraszam.**
Do you speak English?	**Czy Pan/Pani mówi po angielsku?**
I don't understand.	**Nie rozumiem.**
I understand.	**Rozumiem.**
I don't know.	**Nie wiem.**
Where is…?	**Gdzie jest…?**
How do I get to…?	**Jak dojechać do…?**
Good morning/day.	**Dzień dobry.** (jen doe-bri)
Good evening.	**Dobry wieczór.** (do-bri vee-a ye-chor)
Please.	**Proszę.** (pro-sha)
Help!	**Pomocy!** (po-mo-tsay)
Where is the toilet?	**Gdzie są toalety?**
May I have…?	**Czy mogę…?**
entrance	**wejście**
exit	**wyjście**
open	**otwarte / cynny**
closed	**zamknięte**
pharmacy	**apteka**
post office	**poczta**
avenue	**Aleja (Al.)**
street	**ulica (ul.)**
city centre	**centrum**
old town	**stare miasto**

M

MAPS

Tourism Information Offices (see page 175) routinely supply visitors with free maps of cities (and regions, often for a nominal fee). There are plenty of more comprehensive maps available, published by PPWK and others. Those driving through Poland may want to purchase a Road Atlas (Atlas Samochodowy).

MEDIA

Newspapers and magazines. *The Warsaw Voice* (www.warsawvoice. pl), published weekly, is probably the most authoritative English-language newspaper. It gives a good insight into Polish politics, business and culture and also has a listings section for tourists. Other papers to look for include *Welcome to Warsaw* (a free information magazine), *Warsaw Insider* (www.warsawinsider.pl) a free quarterly with cultural listings, and the ever-growing series of *In Your Pocket* mini-guides which have lots of listings and opinionated information (Warsaw, Kraków, Gdańsk, Wrocław, Łódź and Poznań editions at differing intervals, also available as iPhone apps). *Kraków Post* (www.krakowpost. com) is an entertaining monthly. Western newspapers, including *The International Herald Tribune*, *Financial Times* and *USA Today*, arrive the day of publication. Others may arrive a day or two late.

Radio and television. Polskie Radio (www.thenews.pl) is transmitted in English streamed over the internet and as podcasts. Even quite modest hotels now offer satellite television with major European and American channels and news programmes.

MONEY

Currency. The unit of currency is the złoty (zł). Coins in circulation include 1, 2 and 5 zł. Banknotes come in denominations of 10, 20, 50, 100 and 200 zł. One złoty equals 100 groszy (gr), which you'll see in 1, 2, 5, 10, 20 and 50 coin denominations.

Currency exchange. Foreign currency can be exchanged (look for the signs marked *kantor*) at the airports and banks, as well as most hotels. *Kantors* only exchange cash and can be very informal-looking places. They offer the best rates (no commission). Your passport is only necessary when changing money at banks. The exchange rate at the time of writing is around 3.2 zł to the US dollar and 5.5 zł to the pound. There is no black market for currency in Poland; any offers from strangers to exchange money should be refused as this will be counterfeit. The Polish word for cash is *gotówka*.

Numbers

zero	**zero**	eleven	**jedenaście**
one	**jeden**	fifteen	**piętnaście**
two	**dwa / dwie**	sixteen	**szesnaście**
three	**trzy**	seventeen	**siedemnaście**
four	**cztery**	eighteen	**osiemnaście**
five	**pięć**	nineteen	**dziewiętnaście**
six	**sześć**	twenty	**dwadzieścia**
seven	**siedem**	thirty	**trzydzieści**
eight	**osiem**	forty	**czterdzieści**
nine	**dziewięć**	fifty	**pięćdziesiąt**
ten	**dziesięć**	hundred	**sto**

Credit cards. Major international credit cards (Visa, MasterCard and American Express) are increasingly accepted in hotels, restaurants and shops, but are not accepted everywhere. In some cases, only one of the above credit cards will be accepted. You are usually unable to pay with a credit card at small supermarkets, museums and minor train stations.

ATMs. Cash machines (bankomat), taking PLUS, Cirrus and most other major credit cards, are widespread in Polish cities and offer competitive international exchange rates. They dispense cash in Polish zł; a few also give cash in euros.

O

OPENING TIMES

Opening times vary, but most businesses in Poland are open 8am–5pm Monday to Friday. Supermarkets, department stores and shopping centres are open 9am–8pm, Monday to Saturday; Sunday, 10am–6pm and sometimes later. Smaller shops are open 10am–6pm Monday to Friday, 9 or 10am–11 or 12 noon Saturday. Some close all day Saturday, and almost all shut on Sunday. 'Non-Stop' signs mean 24-hour shopping.

Banks are generally open 9am–6pm Monday to Friday. Museums are usually closed on Monday, and are open 10am–5pm Tuesday to Sunday, but museum hours can vary enormously with some closing for lunch and others having opening hours that change with the months of the year.

P

POLICE *(policja)* (see also Crime & Safety and Emergencies)

Police emergency, tel: 997 or 112 from a mobile.
Warsaw Police Headquarters: ul.Puławska 148/150 (tel: 022 621 02 51).

police station	**posterunek policji**

POST OFFICES *(poczta)*

The Central Post Office (Urząd Pocztowy Warszawa 1) in Warsaw (ul. Świętokrzyska 31–33, tel: 022 505 3316) is open 24 hours a day. Other useful branches are at Targowa Street (ul. Targowa 73, also 24 hours a day, tel: 022 590 0313), on ul. Marszałkowska 26 (Mon–Fri 8am–8pm; tel: 022 629 3236) and Old Market Square (Rynek Starego Miasta 15, 8am–8pm Mon–Fri, Sat 9am–4pm; tel: 022 831 2333).

In Kraków, the main Post Office is just east of the Planty (ul. Westerplatte 20, tel: 012 421 03 48; open Mon–Fri 8am–8pm, Sat 8am–

2pm). For post out of hours try the branch opposite the train station at (ul. Lubicz 4; tel: 012 422 91 68; open 24 hours for stamps, post and money transfers).

International postcards and letters to Europe cost 2.40 zł; to the US and Canada, 2.50 zł.

DHL, TNT and UPS all have offices in Warsaw and in Kraków.

letter	**list**
stamp	**znaczek**
air mail	**poczta lotnicza**

PUBLIC HOLIDAYS

1 January	New Year's Day
6 January	Epiphany
March/April	Easter Sunday and Easter Monday
1 May	Labour Day
3 May	Constitution Day
May/June	Pentecost (7th Sunday after Easter)
June	Corpus Christi (9th Thursday after Easter)
15 August	Feast of the Assumption
1 November	All Saints' Day
11 November	Independence Day
25 December	Christmas Day
26 December	St Stephen's Day

R

RELIGION

Nearly all native Poles are Roman Catholic, and as many as 80 percent are practising Catholics. The late Pope John Paul II was a Cardinal and Archbishop of Kraków before becoming the head of the Catholic Church. Mass is said in Polish.

Other minority faiths, notably Protestant, Eastern Orthodox and Jewish, are represented in Poland. Tourism Information Offices should have a list of services held in English and other languages (infrequent).

T

TELEPHONES *(telefon)*

Public telephones. Public telephones are rare in Poland. If you can actually find one, it works using prepaid cards bought from any shop or kiosk selling sweets and cigarettes.

Mobile phones. Avoid roaming costs by putting a local prepaid SIM card in your mobile phone. Several companies now offer start-up packages for less than 10zł, with top-up cards costing 5zł and upwards. Both can be bought from shops and kiosks around the city as well as the airport, bus and railway stations.

Making the call. To call Poland from outside the country, dial your international access code followed by 48 for Poland and the subscriber number minus the initial 0. If you're calling within the country from anywhere in Poland on a landline you simply dial the 10-digit number include the area code beginning with zero. The same applies for calling a landline from a Polish mobile with the exception of Plus GSM, which requires the dropping of the first 0. To get a line out of Poland, dial 00 plus the country code. Mobile telephone numbers have 10 digits and begin 06.

National Operator: 912

International Operator: 901

International dialling code for Poland: 48

Local and regional directory assistance: 913

International directory assistance: 908

Area codes:

Gdańsk/Gdynia/Sopot	058
Kraków	012

Łodź	042
Poznań	061
Toruń	056/055
Warsaw	022
Zakopane	018
Zamość	084

TIME ZONES

All of Poland is in the same time zone, Central European Time, or Greenwich Mean Time + 1 hour (or US Eastern Standard Time + 6 hours). As in the rest of Europe, the clocks go forward one hour on the last Sunday of March and back again on the last Sunday of October.

New York	London	**Warsaw**	Jo'burg	Sydney	Auckland
6am	11am	**noon**	1pm	10pm	midnight

TIPPING

Tipping is the norm in Poland but not obligatory. It's customary to leave 10–15 percent at restaurants and round up the bill at bars. Some restaurants may add on a 10 percent tip. Porters, maids and tourist guides also expect tips.

bill/check	**rachunek**

TOILETS

In Poland public toilets (toaleta publiczna) can be few and far between. A small charge (1–2 zł) is common, and even cafés may still charge patrons for use of their facilities. Men's rooms are commonly denoted by triangle symbols; women's rooms are denoted by circles.

men's room	**męski (panowie)**
women's restroom	**damski (panie)**
free	**wolny**
occupied	**zajęty**

TOURIST INFORMATION

Polish tourist information centres range from desks tucked away in the corners of obliging travel agencies, to dedicated buildings complete with interactive maps. The most popular tourist cities such as Kraków, Warsaw and Gdańsk have many branches. Note that there is a difference between official tourist information centres and the many agencies that label themselves 'tourist information' and exist mainly to sell guided tours and tickets. As well as being able to help you plan your itinerary, most places also offer help and advice on accommodation, car hire, the best places to eat authentic local food as well as a whole host of other useful services. Below are details of a few of the tourist information offices in the key cities.

Warsaw. You will find tourist information points at Chopin Airport (Terminal A, exit 2); Palace of Culture and Science (pl. Defilad 1, from ul. Emilii Plater, between Kongresowa Hall and Museum of Technology); Warszawa Centralna (the Central Railway Station's main hall); Rynek Starego Miasta 19–21a and Kordegarda (ul. Krakowski Przedmieście 15–17). For general tourist information, tel: 022 19431 or see www.warsawtour.pl.

Kraków. The offical Kraków City Tourist Office has several InfoKraków branches throughout the city, mainly open daily 9am–7pm. Cloth Hall, Main Market Square 1-3 (tel: 012 433 73 10; www.cracow.travel.pl and www.krakow.pl).

Gdańsk. Again, there are several Centrum Informacji Turystycznej, at the airport and in the city: ul. Długi Targ 28–29 (058 301 4355, www.gdansk4u.pl); ul. Długa 45 (tel: 058 301 1343; www.pttkgdansk.pl) and others, www.gdansk.pl.

Łódź. Centrum Informacji Turystycznej (ul. Piotrkowska 87, tel: 042 638 5956), www.uml.lodz.pl), at the airport and other points in the city.

Poznań. Centrum Informacji Miejskiej (ul. Ratajczaka 44, tel: 061 19431 or 061 851 9645) and Tourism Information Centre (Stary Rynek 59-60, tel: 061 852 6156), www.cim.poznan.pl.

Official web addresses for other destinations listed in this book:

Auschwitz www.auschwitz.org.pl

Kazimierz Dolny www.kazimierzdolny.pl

Malbork www.visitmalbork.pl

Sopot www.sopot.pl

Toruń www.torun.pl

Wieliczka www.wieliczka.eu

Zakopane www.promocja.zakopane.pl

Zamość www.zamosc.pl

For general information before you leave home, contact the Polish National Tourist Office :

UK: Polish National Tourist Office, Westgate House, West Gate, London W5 1YY; tel: 0300 303 1812; www.poland.travel.

US: Polish National Tourist Office, 5 Marine View Plaza, Hoboken, New Jersey, NJ 07030; tel: 201 420 99 10; www.poland.travel.

TRANSPORT

Local transport

Most Polish cities have well-developed systems of public transport that include buses and trams (and in the case of Warsaw, a single Metro, or subway, line, with a second due to open in 2014 and a third planned).

In Warsaw (www.ztm.waw.pl), buses run from 5am to 11pm; night buses from 11.15pm to 4.30am. Tickets (valid on buses, trams and the Metro) can be purchased at kiosks with a green-and-yellow Ruch logo, and you can also buy a ticket directly from the driver for a slightly higher price. Lines beginning with the number 1, 2, or 3 stop at all stops, those beginning 4 and 5 are speedier.

In Kraków, there are many tram lines and many more bus lines (www.mpk.krakow.pl). They run from 5am to 11pm. You can purchase single-trip tickets, one-hour tickets, one-day and one-week passes. Some night buses (numbers always start with 6) run about once an hour from midnight mostly through the city centre (they stop under the Central Station).

Buses (autobus). Validate your ticket upon boarding to avoid an on-the-spot fine. There is a wide range of ticket prices, with time-limited tickets allowing passengers to change lines within the stated time. Signal that you want to get off by pressing the bell. Roadworks and the rapid modernisation of Polish cities mean that routes are subject to change.

Trams (tramwaj). Trams, or streetcars, cover large networks in most Polish cities; some run throughout the night. In Warsaw, there's an Old Town tram that begins and ends its route at Castle Square, taking a 30-minute guided trip through the Old and New Towns. Many of the T trams are vintage and a Chopin tram, playing the music of the Polish composer, also plies this route.

Taxis (taksówka). Taxi fares depend on the length of the journey and the rate, which changes according to the time of day. Night and weekend rates are higher. Official licensed taxis are clearly badged inside and out and have a roof-light. Unofficial taxis are common, and tend to gather at airports and train stations. If you want a taxi, ask your hotel to call one for you. For taxi company details, *see page* 157. Hailing a cab is not recommended.

Subway or underground (Metro). The Metro in Warsaw (www.metro.waw.pl) operates a single line that runs through the city centre from Młociny station to the southern suburb of Kabaty (near Ursynów). It functions daily 5am–midnight (to 2.30am Fri and Sat), with trains every 3–4 minutes during rush hour, every 8 minutes during off-peak hours.

Transport around the country

Buses/coaches (autobus). The main bus station in Warsaw is Warszawa Zachodnia (Warsaw West, Al. Jerozolimskie 144, tel: 0703 403

330). Kraków's main bus station is behind the train station (ul Bosacka 18, tel: 012 411 8019). Gdańsk's bus station is Dworzec PKS (ul. 3 Maja 12, tel: 58 306 48 43) adjacent to the train station.

The national bus service PKS (www.pksbilety.pl) has the most extensive network of bus routes throughout the country.

For bus information, tel: 0703 40 33 30.

Trains (pociąg). With more than 26,500km (16,450 miles) of railway lines, the Polish railway network covers the whole country, making trains by far the most common and best way to travel between major cities. The exception is short journeys, when buses can be faster (Kraków to Zakopane, for example). Warsaw has three big railway stations; most international trains arrive at Warszawa Centralna (Al. Jerozolimskie 54), while others go to Warszawa Zachodnia (Al. Jerozolimskie 144), which has good interchanges and Warszawa Wschodnia (ul. Lubelska 1) across the river in Praga. Smaller stations, mostly on the edges of the city, handle regional routes.

Kraków's main railway station is Kraków Dworzec Główny (Pl. Dworcowy 1, tel: 012 9436); it handles international and inter-city routes. Gdańsk's railway station is Gdańsk Główny (ul. Podwale Grodzkie 1, tel: 058 9436); the fast SKM commuter train connects the Tri-city area, leaving every 10 minutes between 6am and 7.30pm and less frequently thereafter.

The rail journey from Warsaw to Kraków takes 3 hours; from Warsaw to Gdańsk, 3 hours 40 minutes; and from Warsaw to Poznań, 3 hours 20 minutes.

Tickets can be purchased at the train station in advance or on board from the conductor (for a surcharge).

For train timetables and information, visit www.pkp.com.pl, www.intercity.pl. Informaton: tel: 022 194 36; from abroad: 22 511 60 03).

| railway station | **dworzec kolejowy** |
| bus stop | **przystanek** |

ticket kiosk (buses/trams)	sprzedaż biletów mpk
reserved seat ticket	miejscówka
departure	odjazd
arrival	przyjazd
Please, a ticket to…	Proszę bilet do…
return ticket	bilet powrotny

V

VISAS AND ENTRY REQUIREMENTS

All visitors need a valid passport to enter Poland. Holders of European Union passports do not need a visa and may stay as long as they please. Visitors holding passports from many other countries, including Australia, New Zealand, Canada and the US may also enter Poland without a visa but their stay may be limited, usually for 90 days. Citizens of South Africa and a few other states will need a visa; check at www.msz.gov.pl. Poland is a member of the Schengen group of countries, meaning that a Schengen Block visa is valid for entry to Poland. Visa applications need to be registered online at www.e-konsulat.gov.pl, where there is more detailed visa information. Minimum visa processing times range from 10 days to a month, depending on the passport held, and can take longer.

Customs restrictions. There is a 10,000-euro limit on the amount of currency you can bring into Poland. Visitors are allowed to bring in duty-free alcohol and tobacco products for personal use only, eg, 800 cigarettes and 10 litres of spirits. Check with your home country how much you can bring back duty-free from Poland. Note that airport checks are fierce.

There are also strict regulations to prevent the export of objects of national heritage, such as works of art and antiques. In most cases, works by living artists and works less than 55 years old are exempt. However, there are exceptions to this rule. Reputable antique and art dealers can help their clients get export permits from the Ministry of Culture and National Heritage. Each region has its own department for the export of works of art. In Warsaw it is: Wojewódzki Urząd Ochrony Zabytków W Warszawie, ul. Nowy Świat 18/2; tel: 022 443 04 40; www.mwkz.pl.

WEBSITES AND INTERNET ACCESS

In Kraków, travellers can access free wi-fi in and around the Main Market Square (Rynek Główny) and in ul. Szeroka in Kazimierz. Accept the Krakow123Internet network and you will be redirected to www.123wifi.eu where you can begin browsing. Look out, too, for the hotspot Cracovia logo signalling free wi-fi at hotels and cafés.

Warsaw has free internet hot spots in the Old Town, on Krakowskie Przedmieście Street, 'Wiech' Passage (pasaż Wiecha) at the back of the 'Wars i Sawa' Shopping Centre and in the Browarna Street area (Powiśle district). Free internet is also available in many city centre cafés.

Here are some useful websites to help you plan your trip to Poland:

www.poland.travel (Polish National Tourist Office)

www.warsawvoice.com.pl (site of English-language weekly)

www.krakow.pl (Kraków site)

www.warsawtour.pl (Warsaw tourist information)

www.gdansk.pl (municipal site)

www.pkp.com.pl (Polish state railway schedules)

YOUTH HOSTELS

There is an extensive network of youth hostels (*schroniska młodzieżowe*) in Poland. Contact the Polish Association of Youth Hostels (ul. Mokotowska 14, Warsaw, tel: 022 849 8128, www.ptsm.org.pl) or the International Student Hostels Accommodation through the ALMATUR Travel Bureau (ul. Kopernika 23, Warsaw, tel: 022 826 2639, www.almatur.pl).

Recommended Hotels

Accommodation for visitors to Poland has improved greatly in recent years, with hotels offering modern facilities, often in beautiful old buildings. However, especially at the mid- to lower-range, choices can be limited. International chains and joint ventures have moved in to replace the former state-run chains that were, not always successfully, privatised, and some new, small, Polish-owned private chains are offering excellent quality. It is always wise to book ahead, particularly for June, July, August and September.

The following guide denotes the rack rate price of a double room with bath/shower in high season (May through October, as well as Christmas) including breakfast and VAT. Hotel room rates are variously quoted in US dollars, euros and Polish złoty – though the bill will ultimately be rendered in złoty. Hotels do not always include breakfast in the price they quote on websites, etc, so you will need to check when booking. All accept major credit cards, except where noted.

Most local tourism information offices will also have lists of private accommodation.

$$$$	over 600zł
$$$	425–600zł
$$	250–425zł
$	below 250zł

KRAKÓW

Cybulskiego Guest Rooms $ *ul. Cybulskiego 6, tel: 012 423 05 32, www.freerooms.pl.* A short walk from Rynek Główny, this is a simple, well-run set of rooms and small apartments, all with private bathrooms and kitchenettes, that has a cheerful cellar breakfast room.

Grand Hotel $$$$ *ul. Sławkowska 5/7, tel: 012 424 0800, www.grand.pl.* A stylish 19th-century Old Town hotel with stained-glass shining on its hallways and classic furnishings, the Grand is one of the most impressive places to stay in Kraków. It offers lavishly furnished rooms and some extremely chic suites with period features. There's also an elegant Belle Époque restaurant.

Guest Rooms Wielopole $$$ *ul. Wielopole 3, tel: 012 422 1475, www.wielopole.pl.* Excellent value accommodation two minutes east of the Old Town; facilities are clean and modern. More of a hotel than a guesthouse. Prices include free high-speed internet connection in every room.

Hotel Copernicus $$$$ *ul. Kanonicza 16, tel: 012 424 3400, www. hotel.com.pl.* On one of Kraków's most atmospheric streets, this is one of the city's grandest hotels. It integrates all modern facilities (including a swimming pool in the vaults) in a marvellously restored 16th-century building just minutes from Wawel Hill. Rooms are very elegant, furnished with well-chosen antiques.

Hotel Eden $$$ *ul. Ciemna 15, tel: 012 430 6565, www.hoteleden.pl.* A friendly, small hotel leading a revival of the historic Jewish quarter, Kazimierz. Simple and modern furnishings in a renovated 15th-century building, with a salt-cave sauna, mikvah (Jewish ritual bath) and offering groups who pre-book kosher food. Good pub, Ye Old Goat, downstairs.

Hotel Francuski $$$$ *ul. Pijarska 13, tel: 012 627 3777, www.orbis. pl.* This handsome, traditional hotel, built in 1912, is on the edge of the Old Town, facing the Planty near the old city wall and the Czartoryski Museum and three minutes' walk from the Rynek. It was bought by the Gessler family from the collapsed Orbis chain at the end of 2011 and the new owners promise to maintain its reputation for luxury and elegance. Wheelchair access.

Hotel Maltański $$$ *ul. Straszewskiego 14, tel: 012 431 0010, www. donimirski.com.* One of a small, boutique hotel chain, this modern and elegant hotel in a renovated 19th-century building is in a quiet location on the southwestern edge of the Planty within walking distance of Wawel Hill and all major sights. Classy rooms, good service and breakfast.

Hotel Pollera $$$ *ul. Szpitalna 30, tel: 012 422 1044, www.pollera. com. pl.* Art lovers will like this traditional 150-year-old hotel the moment they enter the lobby. A stained-glass window by Kraków artist Stanisław Wyspiański hangs over the staircase. Rooms are old-fashioned but nicely equipped for the price. Close to the Opera House and Market Square.

Hotel Polski Pod Białym Orłem $$$ *ul. Pijarska 17, tel: 012 422 1144, www.podorlem.com.pl.* A pleasant, medium-sized, quiet hotel, near St Florian's Gate, with wi-fi and all mod cons, yet proud of its historic inheritance, from the fossils in the lobby floor to its 19th-century friezes.

Hotel Rezydent $$$ *ul. Grodzka 9, tel: 012 429 5410, www.rezydent. krakow.pl.* A great location if you want to be in the thick of things: on the street with the most foot traffic leading off the Market Square. Appropriately ancient on the outside, fresh and modern on the inside. Triples and a huge apartment for four available.

Hotel Saski $$ *ul. Sławkowska 3, tel: 012 421 4222, www. hotelsaski. com.pl.* An enviably located old-style hotel in a 16th century building, smack in the middle of the Old Town, on one of its nicest streets. Rooms are either very traditional and very frilly, or rather modern.

NorPol Apartments $$$ *ul. Szlak 50/115, tel: 0501 036 709, www. norpol-apartments.com.* A range of good-looking, non-smoking apartments from matchbox-size to palaces throughout the city centre, which offer a range of add-ons, including airport pick-up and day trips. Long-term rental is also available. A good choice for anyone looking for self-catering.

Pod Różą $$$$ *ul. Floriańska 14, tel: 012 424 3300, www.hotel.com. pl.* One of Kraków's most popular Old Town hotels is this mid-size charmer in the centre of everything. The 14th-century building has been renovated in a traditional style, keeping the arched ceilings and chandeliers, adding modern technology where necessary.

Pod Wawelem $$ *pl. Na Groblach 22, tel: 012 426 2626, www.ho-telpodwawelem.pl.* Simple yet comfortable accommodation in a modern building with friendly, helpful staff is made special by its stunning riverside location at the foot of Wawel hill, within easy walking distance of both the Old Town and Kazimierz. In summer the rooftop bar offers an unparalleled view.

Stary $$$$ *ul. Szczepańska 5, tel: 012 384 0808, www. stary.hotel.com. pl.* Everything is impeccable here, from a renovation job that perfectly blends 14th-century and contemporary style, to staff who are genuinely pleased to help. To top it all, a rooftop bar with a splendid view of the Rynek provides a wonderful place to unwind during the summer.

ZAKOPANE

Hotel Belvedere $$$$ *ul. Droga do Białego 3, tel: 018 202 1200, www.belvederehotel.pl.* Modern hotel built in the traditional, local style, with a sports centre including a swimming pool, squash court and gym. Three restaurants, a café and two bars provide plenty of choice. Within walking distance of Zakopane's centre.

Hotel Litwor $$$–$$$$ *ul. Krupówki 40, tel: 018 202 4200, www.litwor. pl.* On a small square off Zakopane's main shopping promenade, this large, handsome traditional hotel is one of the choicest places to stay in town. It has a delightful lobby bar, great restaurant, nicely furnished rooms, an indoor swimming pool and fitness centre with sauna.

Villa Marilor $$$$ *ul. Kosciuszki 18, tel: 018 200 0670, www.hotel-marilor.com.* A traditional, elegant country-house hotel in a central location, with a tennis court and large garden. The restaurant serves Polish and European cuisine.

ZAMOŚĆ

Arkadia $ *Rynek Wielki 9, tel: 084 638 6507, www.arkadia.zamosc.pl.* An enviable location, right on one of Poland's finest Renaissance market squares, this tiny hotel may lack wi-fi but is nevertheless excellent value.

Hotel Orbis Zamojski $$$ *ul. Kołłątaja 2–6, tel: 084 639 2516, www.accorhotels.com.* This hotel, occupying six nicely renovated 16th-century townhouses next to the Town Hall on the magnificent Market Square, still carrying the Orbis name, is part of the Accor chain and is one of its better efforts. Stylishly modern, but respectful of the original architecture, the buildings are connected by lovely interior courtyards.

KAZIMIERZ DOLNY

Dom Architekta $$ *Rynek 20, tel: 081 883 5544, www.kazimierzdolny.eu.* Owned by the Polish Union of Architects, who have taken a minimal approach to traditional style, in a great location on the Market Square.

Hotel Zajazd Piastowski $ *ul. Słoneczna 3, tel: 081 889 0900, www.zajazdpiastowski.pl.* A large and pleasant chalet-style hotel, set in countryside a few kilometres beyond the town centre. Swimming pool and bicycle rental, horseback riding.

Willa Agnieszka $ *ul. Krakowska 41 A, tel: 081 882 0411, willaagnieszka.pl.* Handily placed for the Rynek yet in leafy surroundings, this modern villa has its own restaurant. A couple of suites have fireplaces, and others balconies overlooking the river. The decor is not the most successful modern take on Polish traditional style.

WARSAW

Agrykola $ *ul. Myśliwiecka 9, tel: 022 622 9100, www.agrykola-noclegi.pl.* This good value hostel near the Łazienki Park and the Ujazdowski Castle is aimed primarily at student sports groups and offers simple accommodation about 3km from the city centre.

Hotel Campanile $$ *ul. Towarowa 2, tel: 022 582 7200, www.campanile.com.pl.* Inside the same huge building as two other hotels, the city-centre air-conditioned Campanile is benefitting from an upgrade taking place throughout the chain. It may be characterless, but for value, service and facilities this one really is very hard to beat.

Hotel Harenda $$$ *Krakowskie Przedmieście 4–6, tel: 022 826 0071, www.hotelharenda.com.pl.* Great location near the university on one of Warsaw's finest streets, a few minutes' walk from the Old Town. Rooms are modern and plainly furnished. There's a lively pub (of the same name) next door.

Hotel Maria $$$ *al. Jana Pawła II 71, tel: 022 838 4062, www.hotelmaria.pl.* A delightful family-run hotel near the Powązki and Jewish cemeteries and within walking distance of the Old Town. Friendly service and nicely furnished modern rooms; an especially good option for those who don't like big corporate hotels. The restaurant offers a good variety of Polish and European dishes and a well-chosen wine list.

Le Royal Méridien Bristol $$$$ *ul. Krakowskie Przedmieście 42–4, tel: 022 551 1000, www.lemeridien.pl.* The most luxurious traditional hotel in Warsaw, this beautiful 1901 Beaux Arts building is elegantly furnished throughout. Within walking distance of the Old Town. Fitness centre, pool, sauna. Great café, restaurant.

Marriott Warsaw $$$-$$$$ *al. Jerozolimskie 65–79, tel: 022 630 6306, www.marriott.com.* Luxurious modern high-rise in the city centre, with 10 restaurants, health club, swimming pool and penthouse cocktail bar.

MDM Hotel $$$ *pl. Konstytucji 1, tel: 022 339 1600, www.hotelmdm. com.pl.* Large hotel centrally located on Constitution Square. The building is typical of 1950s Polish architecture, and the standard décor is rather anonymous, but rooms are large and it's a fair deal for the location.

Nathan's Villa $ *ul. Piękna 24–6, tel: 022 622 2946, www.nathansvilla. com.* This small hostel chain has acquired a legendary status. Accommodation is simple, modern and neat as you'd expect, but, best of all, it's right in the heart of town, just off the main Marszałkowska drag.

Polonia Palace Hotel $$$ *al. Jerozolimskie 45, tel: 022 318 2800, www.poloniapalace.com.* One of Warsaw's oldest hotels, immaculately restored with a Belle Époque restaurant and modern facilities, in a city centre location.

Sheraton Warsaw $$$$ *ul. Prusa 2, tel: 022 450 6100, www.sheraton.com.pl.* The hotel of choice for international business travellers, the very modern and elegant Sheraton is located halfway between Łazienki Park and the Old Town. Rooms are luxuriously appointed, and 'executive rooms' are completely outfitted with work facilities. Excellent gym, restaurants, services.

GDAŃSK

Dom Aktora $$ *ul. Straganiarska 55, tel: 058 301 5901, www.domaktora.pl.* This low-key pension in the heart of the Main Town has a reputation as a boarding house for actors and theatre people. Rooms are utterly simple, but very clean and the art on the walls is for sale.

Hotel Hanza $$$$ *ul. Tokarska 6, tel: 058 305 3427, www.hotelhanza.pl.* One of Gdańsk's most luxurious options in the Main Town. On the waterfront (some rooms have river views), this modern hotel is also just minutes from the Long Market. Attractive and luxurious rooms with a clean aesthetic décor. Hairdressing salon and fitness centre with spa. Very good restaurant and cocktail bar.

Mercure Hevelius Gdańsk $$$$ *ul. Heweliusza 22, tel: 058 321 0000, www.mercure.com.* Within walking distance of the Old Town, this comfortable modern hotel has a good restaurant, beauty salon, massage parlour, solarium and nightclub. Being a high-rise, the hotel provides great views from the guestrooms.

Minihotel Abak $ *ul. Beethovena 8, tel: 058 306 2990, www.abak.gda.pl.* A bit of a trek from the city centre up a long steep hill, this superb value guesthouse provides clean, albeit basic accommodation with a communal kitchen and the facility to have restaurant food delivered to your room. Possibly the best budget option in the city.

Scandic Hotel Gdańsk $$$$ *ul. Podwale Grodzkie 9, tel: 058 300 6000, www.scandichotels.com.* This large chain hotel (formerly the Holiday Inn) is just across from the Gdańsk railway station, and close to the highlights of the Main Town, the Old Town and the now-quiet shipyards. Good service, quality business facilities, standard but well-equipped Scandinavian-style rooms.

SOPOT

Pensjonat Wanda $$$ *ul. Poniatowskiego 7, tel: 058 550 3037, www.bws-hotele.pl.* Perfectly located by the beach and near the pier, this pension occupies a period building, with sauna and solarium, and has its own restaurant. Room service is also available

Sofitel Grand Hotel $$$$ *ul. Powstancόw Warszawy 12–14, tel: 058 520 6000, www.sofitel.com.* Most appropriately named, this impressive red-roofed hotel, a 1927 Art Nouveau landmark, sits facing the Gdańsk Bay in the chic seaside resort of Sopot. The hotel is refined but not pretentious. A surprisingly good deal.

TORUŃ

Hotel Petite Fleur $$$ *ul. Piekary 25, tel: 056 621 5100, www.petitefleur.pl.* A cosy little hotel in the heart of Toruń's Old Town, just two blocks from the Market Square. The accommodation is spread over two elegant Renaissance burgher's houses and has retained numerous period features. Rooms are large and comfortable. Very good restaurant downstairs in the cellar.

Hotel Pod Orłem $$ *ul. Mostowa 17, tel: 056 622 5025, www.hotel. torun.pl.* Large for the tiny Old Town, this functional hotel near St Mary's Church is a perfectly fine place to stay, though it doesn't aim much higher than that. Decent restaurant.

Hotel Zajazd Staropolski $$ *ul. Żeglarska 10–14, tel: 056 622 6060, www.gromada.pl.* One of the best options in the Old Town, between the Copernicus Museum and St Mary's Church, on an interesting street that leads to the river. Comfortable and friendly to pets as well as humans. Well-equipped rooms, with simple modern furniture are spread between three handsome townhouses. Good restaurant.

BYDGOSZCZ

Hotel Brda $$$ *ul. Dworcowa 94, tel: 052 585 0100, www.hotelbrda. com.pl.* A towering, Communist-era beauty providing a choice of both renovated and Cold War-feel rooms, free wireless internet and friendly staff, between the train station and the Old Town. Ideal for those looking for the authentic small town Polish experience.

POZNAŃ

Brovaria $$$ *Stary Rynek 73–4, tel: 061 858 6868, www.brovaria.pl.* With views over the Old Market Square, this hotel combines stylish modernity with historic architecture. Good restaurant and bar with its own brewery.

HP Park Hotel $$ *ul. abpa A. Baraniaka 77, tel: 061 874 1100, www. hotelepark.pl.* A well-equipped, modern hotel on the banks of Lake Malta, about 4km (2.5 miles) south of Poznań's city centre. Perfect for trade-show attendees. Excellent, friendly service.

INDEX

Berlitz pocket guide

Poland

Fourth Edition 2012
Reprinted 2014

Written by Neil Schlecht
Updated by Renata Rubnikowicz
Edited by Rebecca Lovell
Picture Researcher: Lucy Johnston
Series Editor: Tom Stainer
Production: Tynan Dean, Linton Donaldson and Rebeka Ellam

Photography credits: Jerry Dennis/APA 19, 20, 27, 29, 79, 85, 95, 101, 111, 118, 119, 121, 133; iStockphoto 32; Kaplan Productions 23; Corrie Wingate/APA 3BR, 4TL, 5TR, 5BR, 5BC, 40, 51, 55, 56, 59, 61, 62, 63, 64, 132, 138, 140, 144, 146; Gregory Wrona/APA 1, 2TL, 2BR, 3CR, 4TR, 4BC, 4-5B, 5TL, 8, 11, 12, 15, 17, 25, 30, 35, 37, 38, 42, 44, 46, 48, 52, 65, 67, 68, 71, 73, 74, 76, 82, 84, 86, 88, 91, 88, 92, 94, 97, 102, 104, 106, 109, 113, 115, 116, 117, 124, 126, 128, 136, 142; Neil Schlecht 80, 98, 123, 130, 134, 141.

Cover picture: 4Corners Images

Every effort has been made to provide accurate information in this publication, but changes are inevitable. The publisher cannot be responsible for any resulting loss, inconvenience or injury.

Contact us

At Berlitz we strive to keep our guides as accurate and up to date as possible, but if you find anything that has changed, or if you have any suggestions on ways to improve this guide, then we would be delighted to hear from you.

Berlitz Publishing, PO Box 7910, London SE1 1WE, England.
email: berlitz@apaguide.co.uk
www.insightguides.com/berlitz

Berlitz®

speaking your language

phrase book & dictionary
phrase book & CD

Available in: Arabic, Cantonese Chinese, Croatian, Czech, Danish, Dutch, English*, Finnish*, French, German, Greek, Hebrew*, Hindi, Hungarian*, Indonesian, Italian, Japanese, Korean, Latin American Spanish, Mandarin Chinese, Mexican Spanish, Norwegian, Polish, Portuguese, Romanian*, Russian, Spanish, Swedish, Thai, Turkish, Vietnamese

*Book only

www.berlitzpublishing.com